PRAISE FOR
A GENESIS OF RELIGIOUS FREEDOM

"Well-researched and beautifully produced, this is the best and most comprehensive volume in print on the Jews of Newport, the Touro Synagogue, and George Washington's famous letter declaring religious liberty the inherent natural right of all Americans."

Jonathan D. Sarna, Joseph H. & Belle R. Braun Professor of American Jewish History, Brandeis University and author of *American Judaism: A History*.

"*A Genesis of Religious Freedom* makes a significant contribution to the public's understanding of Newport's important history as the colonial center of religious tolerance and highlights the role that its Jewish community played in the development of the economic and social fabric during the colonial period. *This book, combined with the presence of the Ambassador John L. Loeb. Jr. Visitors Center, gives historians and interested citizens a much deeper understanding of the importance that Newport's Jewish community played in the birth of our nation.*"

Thomas P. I. Goddard, Chairman of the Board, Newport Historical Society

"As a descendant of Roger Williams, Rhode Island's founder who helped establish religious freedom in America, I welcome this thoughtful volume. *The book documents the contributions of colonial Jewish Newport's community in expanding the traditions Williams established. I salute my good friend John L. Loeb, Jr. for publishing this handsome and lively work, and for sustaining the memory of his forebears buried in the famed Colonial Jewish Burial Ground which can still be visited in the heart of modern Newport.*"

John Jermain Slocum Jr., former President and Chairman of the Board, Newport Preservation Society, Inc.

Touro Synagogue, viewed from the southeast, circa 1818.
The steeple of the Baptist Church is in the background.

A GENESIS OF RELIGIOUS FREEDOM:
THE STORY OF THE JEWS OF NEWPORT, RI AND TOURO SYNAGOGUE

Including Washington's Letter of 1790

MELVIN I. UROFSKY

This work was published with the generous support of:
The David Berg Foundation
Furthermore: a program of the J. M. Kaplan Fund
and Ambassador John L. Loeb Jr.

Design and layout by
Gill Fishman Associates
and
Scott Citron Design

Contributing Editor, David M. Kleiman (1954-2015)

Prepared for publication by Heritage Muse, Inc.™, New York for
The George Washington Institute for Religious Freedom®

ISBN 971-939706-00-3 (paperback)
ISBN 978-1-939706-01-0 (Kindle)
ISBN 978-1-939706-02-7 (ePub)

Printed in the United States of America
Second Edition

GEORGE WASHINGTON INSTITUTE FOR RELIGIOUS FREEDOM®
50 BROAD STREET, SUITE 1137, NEW YORK, NY 10004
WWW.GWIRF.ORG

COVER PHOTOS:
George Washington Portrait
[left] Ambassador John L. Loeb Jr. Visitors Center
[middle] Touro Synagogue
[right] Visitors Center Annex
[back cover] Touro Synagogue and the new Loeb Gates [2012]

{ TABLE OF CONTENTS }

A Personal Letter from Ambassador John L. Loeb Jr.

Ambassador John L. Loeb Jr.

*Left: Main doors and archway to the
Loeb Visitors Center.*
*The archway carving and other elements of the façade were
carved by the artists of the John Stevens Shop in Newport. The
same shop had provided stone-workers to build the synagogue
in 1760-1762.*

Dear Reader,

The history of Newport's Jewish Community may
not be entirely new to American history buffs, but
in general, few Americans know how meaningful a
role this small group of colonial citizens played in the
vanguard of those who established our country's religious freedom.

Our book had its genesis back in 2003 when I invited
Professor Melvin Urofsky, a noted American histori-
an, to provide research to assure historical accuracy of
exhibits for what became, in 2009, the Loeb Visitors
Center on the campus of Touro Synagogue in Newport,
Rhode Island.

The original work of Professor Urofsky for the Visitors
Center exhibits was so thorough in its research, and so
readable, that I began almost immediately to think he
should write a full length book, using his original work
as a springboard—expanding, updating, and using
new information as well as pictures and graphics that
had become available. That seedling idea has become
a reality as this first full-length history of the Jewish
community of Newport and Touro Synagogue written
since the publication, in 1936, of Rabbi Morris Gutstein's *History of the Jews of Newport*. This current book
is published under the aegis of the George Washington
Institute for Religious Freedom.

What inspired my founding of both the George Washington Institute and the Loeb Visitors Center also
fueled my enthusiastic support for this publication. I
hope my letter will whet your appetite for this history
of the 18th-century Newport Jews, and at the same
time make you hungry to know more about an ambi-
tious educational program to encourage tolerance and

acceptance undertaken by the George Washington Institute for Religious Freedom.

Before going further, I would like to tell you a story. It takes place in the fall of 1945 towards the end of World War II. It is about a boy sent to boarding school in 1939 when he was only nine. He is now fifteen. His high school is large, with a mostly American, all white-male student body whose families are well-to-do and well-educated. There are few minorities in this school—only five foreigners (refugees from Europe) and two American Jews, one of whom is this boy.

Saturday night is movie night, and the whole student body attends. The first newsreel pictures of the German concentration camps appear on the screen—horrible, disturbing images of the dead and the near-dead—emaciated men, women, and children in degrading striped uniforms. The pictures take that young boy's breath away.

What happens next completely knocks the wind out of him—the entire student body cheers and hoots. Afterwards, as they leave the auditorium, a group of classmates approach him and sneer, "Well, we don't like Hitler, but at least he's killed the Jews."

That boy was me.

I was stunned. I had thought we were all Americans and that our religion didn't matter as long as we were good Americans. After all, my Grandmother Adeline Moses Loeb had colonial ancestors going all the way back to before the Revolutionary War—in fact to 1697. Moreover, she was a member of the Daughters of the American Revolution!

My experience that terrible night of the Holocaust newsreel fired my lifelong quest to find the basis for hatred of the Jews. As an adult I have sought peace in my own heart and explored ways to teach young people how to live with more than tolerance—to live with warmth and understanding of people whose backgrounds and beliefs are different from one's own. And this brings me to another story.

The George Washington Letter of 1790

Years ago, as a much younger man seeking to learn what our founding fathers thought about God and religion, I came upon an extraordinary letter President George Washington wrote in 1790 to the little Hebrew Congregation in Newport, Rhode Island. I had never before heard of that letter and discovered that practically nobody I knew at the time had ever heard of it either!

George Washington is not usually thought of as a political philosopher, but when I first read his courageous stand, it moved me tremendously:

> *The citizens of the United States of America have a right to applaud themselves for having given to mankind examples of an enlarged and liberal policy—a policy worthy of imitation. All possess alike liberty of conscience and immunities of citizenship."*

This letter of our first president has had a transformative impact on my thinking and my life. In the sentence that means the most to me Washington says:

> *It is now no more that toleration is spoken of as if it was by the indulgence of one class of people that another enjoyed the exercise of their inherent natural rights.*

By moving beyond the idea of religious toleration and defining religious observance as an "inherent natural right," Washington distilled the essence of American religious freedom: the right of everyone to worship according to his or her conscience—indeed, the right not to worship at all!

The Story Behind the Letter

There is a significant story behind Washington's remarkable letter. Rhode Island had been the last to ratify the Constitution, (a slowness that had piqued the president). Nevertheless, when they finally did sign, he overcame his annoyance and decided to make a goodwill visit to the state, starting at Newport, which was Rhode Island's capital at the time. Sailing from New York City (then the new nation's capital), he and his entourage anchored their little packet ship on Newport's bustling waterfront on the morning of August 17, 1790. Later that day they attended a formal dinner.

Moses Seixas presents a Letter from the Hebrew Congregation of Newport, RI to President George Washington.

The next morning, notables and officials of that city and representatives from various civic groups jockeyed for the honor of presenting letters of welcome to the president. Among them was the leader of Newport's Hebrew Congregation, Moses Seixas.[1] His letter was one of only four presented to the president that morning. The Seixas welcome on behalf of the Jewish community poured out gratitude to the president for his courageous leadership in time of war and for agreeing to serve as head of the newly reorganized national government.

The eloquent Seixas letter expressed the hope that this new national administration would accord all of its citizens respect, rights, and tolerance, whatever their background or religious beliefs. Seixas' words so moved the president that, when he responded only a few days later with a letter, Washington went well beyond the hope Seixas had expressed for acceptance of Jews and other minorities. Washington issued a clarion call that echoes down to us more than two centuries later:

> ..., happily the Government of the United States, which gives to bigotry no sanction, to persecution no assistance, requires only that they who live under its protection should demean themselves as good citizens in giving it on all occasions their effectual support.

Washington's promise of full liberty of conscience regardless of religious background was made courageously in advance of the ratification of the Bill of Rights—perhaps with the intent of promoting its adoption by the States. The first ten amendments to the Constitution were indeed ratified in December of 1791, a little more than a year after Washington's magnificent statement to the Hebrew Congregation in Newport.

The amendments established our most sacred rights, the first of which reads:

> Congress shall make no law respecting an establishment of religion, or prohibiting the free exercise thereof; or abridging the freedom of speech, or of the press; or the right of the people to assemble, and to petition the government for a redress of grievances.

When this amendment passed, freedom of religion and separation of church and state, born in colonial Rhode Island, became the fundamental law of the land.

The George Washington Institute for Religious Freedom

Our first president's letter of 1790 to the Hebrew Congregation is as important as any document in the history of the United States. It contains only 337 words, but its key phrases define succinctly, yet with great eloquence, America's most significant freedom. I credit his letter—coupled with my memories of the painful confrontation with my schoolmates that awful night of the Holocaust newsreel—as my motivation and inspiration for founding the George Washington Institute for Religious Freedom (www.gwirf.org).

Our mission is to encourage and motivate this country's teachers to educate their students to more fully understand and appreciate our American freedoms—especially the critical importance of religious freedom and the separation of church and state, the very bedrock of our democracy. To expand the scope of our outreach, we partner with like-minded national organizations

1. Moses Seixas, an ancestral blood cousin of mine, actually presented two letters to President George Washington. Both Washington and Seixas were Master Freemasons, so the first letter was presented as Freemason to Freemason. The second letter was written on behalf of the Hebrew Congregation of Newport.

Religious Freedom and the Washington Letter Exhibit. Facsimiles of both the Seixas and Washington letters are on display with interactive workstations to explore the letters, their history, content, and context in America.

such as Facing History and Ourselves, First Freedom Center of Virginia, and the Bill of Rights Institute.

The Loeb Visitors Center

An opportunity opened in 1997 to further the message of tolerance and to promulgate the George Washington Letter. That year, a few members of Congregation Jeshuat Israel at Touro Synagogue approached me, describing their hope that a visitors center could be built on the Touro campus. Would I help? I did and undertook the project in 1998. Twelve years later the Center was my gift to the congregation and the community. As far as I know, it is the first freestanding visitors center ever erected for a living house of worship. There are no visitor centers at Westminster Abbey in London, at St. Patrick's Cathedral in New York, at the great synagogues in Amsterdam and London, nor at the al Aqsa Mosque in Jerusalem.

When the synagogue was dedicated in 1763, it would have been a prominent feature of the town's skyline seen by visitors as ships entered Newport's harbor. Standing on the hill and overlooking the Colony House, it was flanked by the steeples of John Clarke's Baptist Church and the Friends (Quaker) Meeting House on the north, and by Trinity Church on the south.

This was unusual, given the traditions of European Jews to hide their houses of worship from public view. Building a highly visible, elegant, public house of Jewish prayer was a grand gesture of confidence by the Newport Jewish community. It clearly showed their status with their neighbors and acceptance by local government.

Today the congregation that worships and celebrates in Touro Synagogue is known as Congregation Jeshuat Israel. Established in the 1880s, they are the spiritual descendants of the several Jewish communities and congregations that came before. The building is known as Touro Synagogue, thanks to the nineteenth-century gifts for maintenance and upkeep of the building given by Abraham and Judah Touro—sons of Isaac Touro, the first spiritual leader of the new synagogue community.

For two centuries Touro Synagogue stood alone on the hill in Newport overlooking the old Colony House and Newport Harbor. Now in the 21st -century, this living house of worship is connected by the Loeb Gates and colorfully re-landscaped Patriots Park directly to the new Visitors Center and the historic Barney House (to be the Center's annex), creating a unified Touro Synagogue historic site and campus.

When the Visitors Center opened in August 2009, David Brussat, a leading Rhode Island architectural critic, pronounced it "Newport's deft new Touro jewel." He wrote in the *Providence Journal*:

> *It is obviously a classical building yet it is unlike any other. No work of classicism could possible depart from canon with greater dignity; hence no building could possibly fit on to a historic street with greater distinction. Embedded in this otherwise ancillary building is the spirit of civic congeniality embodied by George Washington's famous words. In tapping its spirit, the Loeb Visitors Center succeeds admirably. The brave new building seems at home in old Newport.*

Speaking of the old town, the George Washington Institute is a proud partner in the consortium of

institutions making up the historic "Newport Old Quarter" of the famous little city. The new look of the Touro campus is drawing more and more visitors to the area every year, bringing a financial boon to the entire neighborhood.

Located at the historic corner of Spring and Touro Streets, you will be greeted warmly by the guides of Touro Synagogue and at the Loeb Visitors Center by our dedicated, knowledgeable docents, eager to answer questions on the four primary exhibits:

- *Touro Synagogue History*
- *The Story of the George Washington Letter*
- *The Origins of Separation of Church and State in RI*
- *Jews in Colonial America*

My Personal Invitation to You

I hope I have engaged your interest through my stories here and that you will not only relish Professor Urofsky's history of Newport's Jews but that you will visit the Loeb Visitors Center and learn to treasure the George Washington Letter as I do. Please do come!

I invite you to visit the two websites that offer a preview of the exhibits, days and hours of operation, and tickets for your visit to the Synagogue and Visitors Center: www.tourosynagogue.org *and* www.loebtouro.org

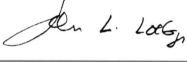

Above: Loeb Visitors Center [right] and the Visitors Center Annex (Barney House) [left].

Loeb Visitors Center [left], Touro Synagogue [center] and Visitor Center Annex (Barney House) [right].

The Portrait Tree.
Perhaps the most popular exhibit is the interactive portrait tree.
The database displays images of over 200 Jewish men, women,
and children painted in the United States and Canada prior
to 1865. The artworks created by major American artists such as
Gilbert Stuart and Thomas Sully, along with short biographies
of the subjects, can also be viewed on the website:
www.loebjewishportraits.org.

Girl in White with Cherries

Rebecca Gratz (1781-1869)

Moses Isaac (1742-1818)

Amelia Lazarus

Isaac Brandon (1760-1853)

Samson Levy Jr. (1781-1831)

Samson Levy

Anna Maria Levy

Augusta L. Feuchtwanger

Major David Salisbury Franks

CHAPTER 1 | An Island of Freedom

Roger Williams (1603–1683).
Credited as the founder of Rhode Island, Williams was amongst the first to write of freedom of conscience and the separation of church and state. With the help of Reverend John Clarke, he obtained the 1663 Royal Charter from King Charles II for the Colonie and Plantation of Rhode Island.

A Map of
New ENGLAND
New YORKE New IERSEY
MARY-LAND & VIRGINIA

Sould by Robert Morden at ye Atlas in
Corn-hill near ye Royal Exchange and by
William Berry at ye Globe between York
House & ye New Exchange in ye Strande
London

{ CHAPTER 1 }

An Island of Freedom

FROM THE SETTLEMENT OF JAMESTOWN IN 1607 UNTIL the American Revolution, the British colonies in North America, with few exceptions, had established churches. In the southern colonies and parts of New York the Church of England enjoyed the same status as it had in the mother country, while in New England various forms of Congregationalism dominated. These colonies consistently discriminated against Catholics, Jews and even dissenting Protestants. In 1656 the General Court of Massachusetts Bay forbade the presence of Quakers in the colony, and should any be found they were to jailed, whipped, and deported.

In the 17th century, when our story begins, religious liberty as we now know it did not exist in Western Europe outside of a small enclave in Holland; freedom of conscience would be a construct of the New World, ultimately embedded as a constitutional right in the First Amendment. The development of that freedom is in many ways the story of the United States itself, and at the heart of the tale is the experiment made by a small group of religious dissenters in Rhode Island. The liberty of conscience they established along the Narragansett Bay would eventually grow into "the first freedom." The religious autonomy enjoyed by dissenters in Rhode Island would attract Jews to Newport, the commercial center of the colony in the 18th century. But the story of Roger Williams, religious liberty in Rhode Island, and the Jews who lived there is far more complicated than is often portrayed. To understand the Jewish experience in

Left: A Map of New England, New Yorke, New Jersey, Maryland & Virginia. [1676] The early British colonies as understood by scholars of the period.

Newport, we have to examine the milieu in which the town's Jews lived—the Rhode Island of the 17th and 18th centuries.

The Reformation that began with Martin Luther on the Continent in the 16th century spread to the British Isles when Henry VIII, once a staunch defender of Catholicism, decided to divorce his first wife in order to marry Anne Boleyn in 1533. England renounced the Catholic Church led by the pope, and in its place established the Church of England with the king as its head. Upon Henry's death, his daughter Mary attempted to restore the old faith, and only her death prevented England from plunging into a bloody civil war. Elizabeth I, the offspring of Henry's union with Anne Boleyn, took the throne in 1558. She supported the Church of England, but did not care to look, as she put it, through a window into men's souls. Providing dissenting religious groups did not disturb the social order, she would allow them to practice and even preach unmolested.

This toleration bought peace in Elizabeth's reign, but it also encouraged religious dissenters who saw the Church of England as too Catholic, too popish, and who wanted to cleanse it of these defects. Known as Puritans, they began a long battle to rid the Church of England of its Romish practices; when they failed at this task, many of them departed for the New World where, in John Winthrop's phrase, they would create a "Zion in the wilderness" in which the true faith could be practiced.

The Puritans who settled in the Boston area, and the more radical Separatists who had earlier landed on Plymouth, did not come to New England seeking religious liberty for any group other than themselves. They believed, as did most Christians at the time, that just as there could be only one king, so there could be only one religion. This tradition goes back to the Old Testament, in which the God of the Hebrews declares "I am the Lord your God, and you shall have no other Gods before Me." (Exodus 20:2-3). The idea of the one true god by definition excludes all other gods, all other religions, all other practices as false and not to be tolerated. If one truly believes in a particular religion, then how can one say that others are free to follow their false gods, false beliefs and false practices? From the time Christianity became the state religion of Rome in the fourth century, the Church demanded that all citizens adhere to its rites, and that those who refused to do so should be compelled to conform, even on pain of death.

An established religion worked hand in glove with the crown, and the great medieval schoolmaster, Thomas Aquinas, saw the necessity of one church and one state cooperating. In a famous analogy, he described church and state as two swords, working in unison to carry out the will of God. Although the Protestant Reformation split the religious unity of Europe, neither Martin Luther nor John Calvin objected to the idea of one true faith, or the necessity of the state enforcing that belief. That idea has remained a powerful one in much of the contemporary world, and even in the United States the notion of religious and secular authorities working together toward a common good has retained great vitality for some. Well after the adoption of the First Amendment, Theophilus Parsons, the chief justice of Massachusetts, wrote:

> *To enforce the moral duties is essential to the welfare of a free state. Religion was made a part of the constitution to co-operate with human institutions, and that religion was Protestant Christianity.*

When a group of Anabaptists in 1681 demanded of the Massachusetts Bay government some toleration on the grounds that the first settlers had fled England to establish a refuge for religious toleration, Rev. Samuel Willard of Boston's Third Church answered that they were "mistaken in the design of our first Planters, whose business was not Toleration; but were professed Enemies of it, and could leave the World professing they died no libertines. Their business was to settle, and (as

much as in them lay) secure Religion to Posterity, according to that way which they believed was of God.

As we noted earlier, the General Court of Massachusetts Bay forbad the presence of Quakers in the colony in 1656, and should any be found they were to be jailed, whipped and deported. But the Quakers were persistent, so the following year the legislature ordered that banished male Quakers who returned should lose one ear; if they returned a second time, the other ear. Females who came back were to be "severely" whipped, and on a third return, male or female should "have their tongues bored through with a hot iron."

But the Quakers kept coming, so in 1658, the General Court prescribed death by hanging, the same penalty imposed upon Jesuits and other Catholic priests who returned after banishment. Between 1659 and 1661 one Quaker woman, Mary Dyer, and three men were indeed hanged upon Boston Common.

As late as 1774, at a time when the colonists were strongly protesting British invasions of their rights, the Reverend Isaac Backus, leader of the Massachusetts Baptists, informed the governor and council that 18 Baptists had been jailed in Northampton, during the coldest part of the winter, for refusing to pay taxes for the support of the town's Congregational minister. That same year, James Madison of Virginia wrote to a friend: "That diabolical, hell-conceived principle of persecution rages among some… There are at this time in the adjacent county not less than five or six well-meaning men in close jail for publishing their religious sentiments, which in the main are very orthodox… So I must beg you to . . . pray for liberty of conscience for all."

Yet from the very beginning of settlement, pressures—many of them emanating from the Mother Country—grew against establishment and conformity. Religion played a major role in the events that led up to the English Civil War, and when the Glorious

Right: Landing of Roger Williams, 1636.
Following his expulsion from Boston, Williams traveled south and landed amongst the Narragansett Indians.

"I desire not that liberty to my selfe which I would not freely and impartially weigh out to all the consciences of the world beside. And therefore I doe humbly conceive that it is the will of the most high, and the expresse and absolute duty of the civill powers to proclaim an absolute freedom…in all the world …that each…person may freely enjoy what worship their soul desireth."

—Roger Williams, *Hireling Ministry None of Christ's (1652)*

Mary Dyer being led to the Scaffold, 1660.

Two Views of Religion

…male Quakers who returned should lose one ear; if they returned a second time, the other ear. Females who came back were to be severely whipped, and on a third return, male or female should 'have their tongues bored through with a hot iron.'

In 1658 the General Court prescribed death by hanging, the same penalty imposed upon Jesuits and other Catholic priests who returned after banishment. Between 1659 and 1661 one Quaker woman, Mary Dyer, and three men were indeed hanged upon Boston Common.

Revolution of 1688 put William and Mary on the throne, they moved immediately to put an end to religious strife. The English Act of Toleration (1689) exempted "their majesties' Protestant subjects, dissenting from the Church of England," from earlier repressive legislation. Parliament, however, excluded Roman Catholics from the Toleration Act's benefits because it considered them subversive, supposedly owing their allegiance not to the Crown but to a foreign power. The Act ignored Jews completely, no doubt because of their small numbers then in England. At about the same time, John Locke provided the ideological basis for this new policy in his *Letters Concerning Toleration*, written between 1689 and 1692. In them Locke adopted the rational thought of the Enlightenment to support the abandonment of government-imposed religious conformity. The royal charter given to Massachusetts Bay in 1691 provided "a liberty of Conscience allowed in the Worshippe of God to all Christians (Except Papists)."

By then this same spirit could be seen in the colonies. As early as 1645 a majority of the deputies in the Plymouth General Court wanted "to allow and maintain full and free tolerance of religion to all men that would preserve the civill peace and submit unto government; and there was no limitation or exception against Turke, Jew, Papist, Arian, Socinian, Nicholaytan, Familist, or any other, etc." The governor refused to allow the resolution to come to a vote, but in stark contrast to neighboring Massachusetts, Plymouth throughout its existence retained a spirit of moderation. In 1649 the Maryland Act Concerning Religion used the expression "free exercise," while in 1670, William Penn issued an influential tract entitled *The Great Case of Liberty of Conscience*, the first time this phrase appeared in American discourse. As more groups entertaining a variety of religious beliefs as well as non-beliefs came to the colonies, it became increasingly difficult to maintain the older notion of one religion tied to the state. Many of the new settlers had no desire to join any church, and by one estimate, at the time of the American Revolution, nine out of ten Americans were unchurched.

Nonetheless, the old spirit died hard. In 1645 the four Puritan colonies of New Haven, Connecticut, Massachusetts and Plymouth formed the United Colonies, primarily for mutual defense against the Indians.

Massachusetts Puritans also wanted the organization to act as a barrier against "error and blasphemy," especially the tolerance for diverse views enjoyed in Plymouth. But if Plymouth appeared lax, the Rhode Island of Roger Williams stood outside the pale.

Williams had been born sometime between 1599 and 1603, the son of a merchant tailor, and educated at Pembroke College, Cambridge, England. Although ordained as a clergyman in the Church of England, he agreed with the Puritans that the reformation in England had not gone far enough to rid the church of its Romish errors. Shunned by the Church of England's hierarchy, he sailed in 1631 to join John Winthrop and the Puritan settlers in Massachusetts. The colony welcomed him warmly, and offered him the pastorate of the first Puritan church in Boston. Although acknowledging the honor, he declined the invitation on the grounds that he believed the Puritans should break openly with the Church of England and go their separate way. He moved from Boston to New Plymouth and later to Salem, where he farmed, traded and preached to the Indians, all the while growing more convinced that the civil authorities lacked any power to compel religious conformity. Only God could command men's consciences, and for the state to force people to honor the Sabbath amounted to "forced worship," which "stinks in God's nostrils."

These views challenged not only prevalent thought but the very legitimacy of established churches, so the Massachusetts elders put him on trial for heresy in 1635 and found him guilty. Because winter had set in, Williams was permitted to continue living in Salem until the spring. When authorities learned, however, that Williams along with 20 others who agreed with his heresy were planning to establish a new settlement on Narragansett Bay, they sent officers to arrest him in January to ship him back to England, where his views would have certainly brought down the wrath of the Crown.

Forewarned, Williams left his ailing wife, and in midwinter found his way to what is now Bristol, Rhode Island, where his friend the Indian chief Massasoit had his winter quarters. In the spring of 1636, with the gift of land from local tribes, Williams established a settlement he named Providence. The town grew slowly.

> *"It hath fallen out sometimes, that both Papists and Protestants, Jews and Turks, may be embarked upon one ship: upon which supposal I affirm, that all the liberty of conscience, that ever I pleaded for, turns upon these two hinges—that none of the Papists, Protestants, Jews, or Turks, be forced to come to the ship's prayers or worship, nor be compelled from their own particular prayers or worship."*
>
> — Roger Williams,
> *Letter to Providence* (1655)

In 1638 it had about 20 families, perhaps 100 persons. Although it doubled in size by 1645, 30 years later it still had only 350 to 400 residents.

While it is true that Williams believed in freedom of individual conscience, one cannot label him as a liberal in the modern sense. He was a man of his own times,

a devout Christian who, as much as John Cotton and other Massachusetts Bay colony Puritan divines, wanted one true religion. Unlike Cotton, however, Williams did not believe that he had found that faith, and so long as he had not, then he could not impose his will on others or force them to believe and worship in a particular manner.

Williams laid out his design for the colony of Rhode Island in 1644, when he published his most famous tract, *The Bloudy Tenent of Persecution, for Cause of Conscience, discussed in A conference betweene Truth and Peace.* Williams envisioned a Christian commonwealth in which all religious persuasions would be allowed to practice freely, while the civil authority rested in a separate realm. No religious body would dominate the civil government, and the magistrates would act according to the dictates of their individual consciences. Such a commonwealth, Williams maintained, could tolerate a great range of individual beliefs, even those of Jews and Muslims. This did not, however, mean that Rhode Island would necessarily welcome a Jewish presence.

In fact, the charter issued to Williams for Rhode Island by Charles II in 1663 made clear that the king envisioned a colony "pursuing, with peaceable and loyal minds, their sober, serious and religious intentions, of godly edifying themselves, and one another, in the holy Christian faith and worship." Nonetheless, the charter did allow:

> *…that noe person within the sayd colonye, atv any tyme hereafter, shall bee any wise molested, punished, disquieted, or called in question, for any differences in opinione in matters of religion, and doe not actually disturb the civill peace of our sayd colony; but that all and everye person and persons may, from tyme to tyme, and at all tymes hereafter, freelye and fullye have and enjoye his and theire owne judgments and consciences, in matters of religious concernments, throughout the tract of lande hereafter mentioned, they behaving themselves peaceablie and quietlie, and not useing this libertie to lycentiousnesse and profanenesse, nor to the civill injurye or outward disturbeance of others…*

Moreover, the charter then emphasized that the colonists had the authority to defend themselves, not only to protect their property and rights, but against "all the enemies of the Christian faith."

What did this mean? One thing we can be fairly sure about is that while Charles II stood prepared to allow a small number of dissidents in a faraway land relatively wide latitude in religious observances, and to forgo having the Church of England established there, he and the royal government still saw Williams and Rhode Island as Christian, and commanded to stay that way. The charter also required that laws of the colony "be comformable to the laws of England," which at the time still disallowed Jewish settlement in the British Isles. On the face of it, this would seem to mandate exclusion of non-Christians, but Williams believed otherwise. In a letter written several years later, he bragged about the exceptional character of the charter:

> *The Kings Matie wincks at Barbadoes where Jews and all sorts of Christians and Antichristian perswasions are free, but our Graunt…is Crowned with the Kings extraordinary favour to this Colony…In wch his Matie declar'd himselfe that he would experimnt whether*

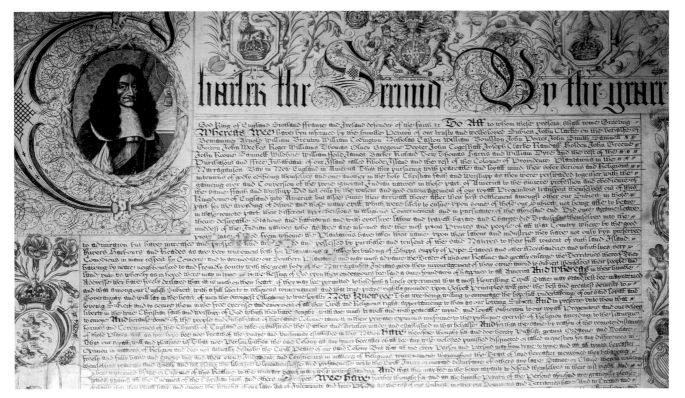

Royal Charter of the Colony of Rhode Island and Providence Plantations (1663).

Civill Govrmnt Could consist with such a Libertie of Conscience.

Williams, a true Christian in his own beliefs, wanted to welcome Jews and others because, in the end, he hoped to convert them to "the principles of Christianity and civility." By residing among good Christians, he thought, Jews, Muslims and other non-Christians would see the error of their ways and convert to the true faith. This claim is fortified by Williams' attitude toward Quakers, who had established a small settlement on Aquidneck Island (site of present day Newport). In a tract entitled *George Foxx Digg'd Out of His Burrowwes* (1676), Williams equated Quaker beliefs with Judaism and Catholicism as a means of discrediting the Friends' theology. God's grace, he wrote, "is a mystery which neither Jews nor Turks, Atheists or Papists, or Quakers know." In the same tract he wrote "Is it not enough that the most High Potter made us Men and Women and not Serpents and Toads, &c., not Pagans, Turks, Jews, Papists &c. but English Protestants."

Williams wanted to establish peace between the various Christian sects, and his references to Jews and Turks may have been no more than a simple rhetorical device. If even Jews and Muslims could live in peace, then so should the different Christian denominations be able to mute their differences for the sake of civil harmony. Williams created a fine balance between the demands of religious conscience and those of the state. Governments had the right to impose and enforce rigorous standards for civil behavior, but they had no right to meddle in matters of conscience. Thus when dealing with Catholics, whom Williams and many other Protestants believed could never be good citizens of a state because they owed their first allegiance to the Pope, the state could require that Catholics wear distinctive clothing and be prohibited from carrying arms, even while allowed to practice their religion freely. This, of course, bears a striking resemblance to how Jews then lived in European ghettos.

In many ways, Williams' views prefigured one of the less attractive attitudes of later American Christians, the desire to convert the Jews. If Jews came to Rhode Island, Williams maintained, they would not be turned away, and neither would they be molested in their religious observances. They could never be full citizens of a Christian commonwealth, however, until they saw the light of the true faith and converted to Christianity. In modern terms, the Jews of Rhode Island would enjoy toleration but not liberty.

The notion of the United States itself as a Christian commonwealth has enjoyed a long tenure in the popular mind. In the 18th and 19th centuries, Protestant Christianity constituted a kind of universal religion among Americans, and a generalized, non-sectarian Protestant culture seemed to be the basis for republican government. Horace Bushnell, a pillar of the Protestant Church, declared that "Protestantism in religion produced republicanism in government." Jurists such as Chancellor James Kent of New York and Supreme Court Justice Joseph Story asserted that Christianity provided the foundation for Anglo-American common law, and Kent went so far as to say that "Christianity was in fact the religion of the country." Later on in the century the distinguished English visitor, James Bryce, declared that "Christianity is in fact understood to be, though not the legally established religion, yet the national religion." As late as 1892, Justice David Brewer could state for a unanimous Court that "this is a Christian nation." During much of the 19th century, Catholics were excluded from the national consensus of Christians, while Jews were basically ignored. In the twentieth century as Catholics and Jews joined the mainstream, the current idiom became that of a "Judeo-Christian nation," although in practice it looked much like the non-denominational Protestantism of the early 19th century.

Other evidence suggests that Williams saw Jews in the abstract, a foil for his own desire to create a unique colony where different Protestant groups could live in peaceful coexistence. When he lived in England he had been close to the great English jurist, Sir Edward Coke, who maintained that as infidels and subjects of the devil, Jews had no rights at law. He seemed to denounce all non-Protestant faiths as "briars, thorns and thistles… in the Garden of the Church," and he made no secret of his desire to convert the Jews. Williams joined other

Protestant millenarians who in the 1650s argued for Jewish readmission to England, but again did so not for the sake of Jewish religious autonomy, but for the chance to convert them.

Williams, it should be noted, had little if any experience with Jews during his lifetime. While a few Jews appeared to have settled in Newport during the 17th century (see next chapter), it is almost certain that no Jews came to Providence until much later, perhaps the early 19th century. To see colonial Rhode Island as a bastion of religious liberty would be to read a later notion of religious freedom backwards in time, to an era when it could not have applied. Williams had a charter from the king to establish a Christian colony, and by the time he secured that charter, both Providence as well as Newport had been split by competing sects, several of whom packed up and left to found new settlements. Jews and Turks could come to Rhode Island—and worship freely there—but the model Williams sought in vain to create was a peaceable kingdom of Christians.

Yet in spite of these Christian underpinnings, Rhode Island even at this time stood in stark contrast to the overt antisemitism that permeated the Mother Country. Jews had been excluded from England for three centuries, and although there were in fact Jews living there during that time, they were ignored. In 1655 Jews were formally readmitted, even though the average Englishman had an extremely negative view of Jews, who were labeled as bloodthirsty and homicidal in intent, blasphemous in religion, and engaged in usury and other disreputable business practices. Englishmen well into the 19th century used the word "Jew" as an insult to suggest a rogue or a cheat. In 1775, when a proper young Scotswoman, Janet Schaw, encountered Jews for the first time, she wrote in her journal that she "could not look on the wretches without shuddering."

What is most important is that Williams and his followers embraced a basic principle that would be at the heart of the religious liberty that later developed in the United States: the separation of church and state. So long as the state maintained an established church, there could be no freedom of religion for those who did not adhere to the teachings of that church. Dissenters might be tolerated, or even welcomed into the colony, but they would know that they would be taxed to support values contrary to their own, and at all times stood in peril that church aligned with state would move against their beliefs, their property, or even their lives. An established church bears the imprimatur of the state, be it a king, a council, or even a democratically elected legislature, and as such its teachings are both explicitly and implicitly declared to be the one true faith.

In arguing for separation, Williams contributed a powerful metaphor that still carries enormous intellectual as well as constitutional significance, and which for many people remains a touchstone in their thinking about church-state relations:

When they have opened a gap in the hedge of or wall of separation between the garden of the church, and the wilderness of the world, God hath ever broken down the wall itself … and made his garden a wilderness, as at this day. And that therefore if He will ever please to restore His garden and paradise again, it must of necessity be walled in peculiarly unto Himself from the world.

For Williams, God's garden—the church—had to be protected against the secular world—the wilderness— or else its unique features would be destroyed. Where some people, such as Thomas Jefferson, wanted to keep church and state separate in order to protect the state from clericalism, Williams wanted separation in order to keep the church pure from the profane nature of the state and secular society.

The importance of separating church and state has always been clear to minorities. However, over time, members of the majority began to understand that while such an alliance worked at times against the interests of both church and state, it did help guarantee individual freedom of conscience. In theocratic societies, the church can demand that the state enforce its orthodoxy, but the state could—as history had shown countless times—demand that the religious authorities enforce its programs as well, sometimes at the expense of religious ideals. No one has articulated this better than Justice Robert H. Jackson, who declared that "if there is any fixed star in our constitutional constellation, it is that no official, high or petty, can prescribe what shall be orthodox in politics, nationalism, religion

or other matters of opinion or force citizens to confess by word or act their faith therein." Long after the disabilities placed on Jews and other minorities in Rhode Island had passed from the scene, this vision of separation of church and state would remain as Roger Williams' greatest legacy.

Although Providence remained the seat of Williams' enterprise and would later be the capital of Rhode Island, Newport dominated the colony's economy until after the American Revolution.

Anne Hutchinson, another independent spirit banished by the Puritans, and a group of followers bought land from the Indians on the northern tip of Aquidneck Island in 1638. But like the Williams settlement at Providence, religious disagreements soon led one group to depart. In 1639 a band of settlers led by Nicholas Easton, William Coddington, and Dr. John Clarke moved to the southern tip of the island and there founded Newport. The document the settlers signed in April, known as the Newport Compact, reflected the same ideas of religious toleration that Roger Williams had preached.

But there were significant differences between Williams and the founders of Newport. The settlers on Aquidneck appear to have been better educated than those who went to Providence, and also far more capitalist-oriented. Williams had little use for business or for material goods, and died in poverty. The Aquidneck settlers, on the other hand, favored economic success, and their individualistic views of religion led to a greater emphasis on individual enterprise. The "Protestant ethic" encouraged success in the market, and prosperous merchants in Newport took their good fortune as a sign that their piety and behavior had pleased God. In many ways individualism in commerce complemented independent thought in religion, both of which sought to be free of interference by the state.

William Coddington had been part of the Boston court that had banished Williams, and he had little use for the Providence settlement. He and his co-founders tried to keep Newport distinct from the Williams group, and in fact proved far more receptive to Quakers than did Williams.

In the eyes of some historians, John Clarke has been unfairly overshadowed by Williams as a defender of religious liberty and a champion of political democracy. It was Clarke, who remained in England for more than a decade, finally obtained the all-important charter from Charles II in 1663. It is Clarke's definition of religious liberty, written into that charter, that is engraved under the marble dome of the Rhode Island state capitol: "To hold forth a lively experiment that a most civil state may stand and best be maintained with full liberty in religious concernment." The Baptist church Clarke established in Newport is the oldest Baptist church in the country.

Clarke and his wife had arrived in Boston in November 1637, and within a short time found himself caught up in the religious dispute between Anne Hutchinson and the more orthodox Puritans. He later wrote: "I thought it not strange to see men differ about matters of Heaven, for I expect no less upon Earth. But to see that they were not able so to bear with each other in their different understandings and consciences as in those utmost parts of the world to live peaceably together [led me to move elsewhere]."

The advantages of a natural harbor led to the economic growth of Newport, while its reputation for tolerance soon brought in a stream of religious groups seeking a haven from persecution. Within a year the population of the settlement had risen from the ten who came with Coddington in the spring to 93. Jews and Quakers arrived about 20 years after the initial settlement, and were soon followed by Seventh Day Baptists, Paedobaptists and other groups; in 1698 the Anglican Church also established a church on the island. The various sects dwelt together in reasonable harmony, and the Presbyterian Samuel Maverick of Boston described the village as "a receptacle for people of several sorts of opinions." Some of the Boston divines had far less charitable views, and labeled Newport a "sewer."

The first settlers farmed the fertile land, instructed in the growing of corn by the Narragansett Indians, but before long they turned to the sea. Because Newport is on an island without a large hinterland for trading, the settlers began fishing, and then moved into the coastal trade. Coddington became one of the first to build

Anne Hutchinson Preaching in Her House in Boston, 1637.

ships large enough to sail up to Boston and down to New Amsterdam (later New York). By 1690 Newport's population had risen to 2,600, of whom half engaged in some aspect of maritime trade. On the eve of the Revolution, Newport was considered one of the five major colonial seaports, along with Boston, New York, Philadelphia, and Charleston, South Carolina.

This is in some ways surprising, since unlike the other four, which had ample room to expand, geography limited Newport's size. The entire island of Aquidneck is only 15 miles from north to south, and varies in width from one to three miles. While there are many coves on the island that would serve as shelter for fisherman as well as smugglers, the only good-size protected harbor is at the southern end at Newport. This lack of productive hinterland would in the end fatally doom Newport's chances of remaining a major seaport.

Prosperity manifested itself in numerous ways. The first settlers hastily erected crude huts to get them through the initial winters, but as soon as possible replaced them with substantial wooden houses, taking advantage of the plentiful nearby forests. By 1680, Newport counted about 400 houses, and the older one-room, end-chimney style gave way to larger homes with central chimneys and two or more rooms on each floor. Prior to King Philip's War (1675–1678) few paupers lived in the town, but several hundred refugees from Providence and other nearby communities fled to Newport seeking safety, and they were taken care of by the Quakers. Many of these poor remained after the fighting had ended, and of these quite a few chose to remain in Newport permanently.

Newport proved welcoming to Jews and to other minorities for two major reasons. First, it subscribed to the notion of religious liberty and separation of church and state, thus creating an atmosphere in which individuals as well as sects could pursue their own religious beliefs and practices without interference from either an established church or temporal magistrates. Second, and just as important, the founders of Newport and those who flocked there afterwards, stood committed to entrepreneurialism. Although elites emerged in the town, no one group ever dominated Newport the way the Brown family and its allies did Providence. Newport had a series of overlapping commercial elites, some of whom had little or nothing to do with politics. The political leaders, while usually well-to-do merchants, did not enjoy great wealth, nor did they prove to be the most innovative in trade. Certainly more than Providence, and more than most New England towns, Newport enjoyed great diversity among its population. By the early 18th century it included not only some prestigious old families, but newer immigrants of different religions and national origins, and probably the largest black population of any place in New England outside of Boston.

The same year of Newport's founding, Roger Williams wrote to John Winthrop: "I heare of a Pinnace [a small ship] to put in to Newport bound for Virginia." During the 1640s and 1650s, a growing Newport merchant fleet traded primarily with New England towns and occasionally New Amsterdam. By the 1660s, however, records indicate that Newport vessels had begun to build up a trade with the West Indies. Here ship owners bought goods that could be sold or exchanged for British-made goods, which would come into Boston

from the Mother Country, and then be trans-shipped to Newport. Despite Newport's growth in population, it still remained a small seaport in terms of volume. Peleg Sanford, Rhode Island's governor in the late 17th century, informed the Board of Trade that the entire colony's shipping was limited to "a few sloopes." Horses and provisions made up the chief exports, while imports were a "small quantity of Barbadoes goods for supply of our families." What Newport lacked, according to Sanford, were men of substance. "We have severall men that deale in buyinge and selling although they cannot properly be called Merchants." Neither Rhode Island in general, nor Newport in particular, had men with the available capital to invest in commercial ventures.

All this began to change toward the end of the 17th century, as people like Sanford (himself a merchant) and Walter Newbury established basic trade routes with the Caribbean islands. Then a new generation of merchants settled in Newport in the first decades of the 18th century from places as diverse as Massachusetts, Virginia, the West Indies and even Europe. Trade, which had been sporadic and limited to a few ports, evolved into a complex system that counted hundreds of voyages annually throughout the New World. One sign of this growth is that in 1720 the number of ships that entered or left Newport amounted to a little over 600; that number grew steadily for the next half-century until it topped 1,600 on the eve of the American Revolution. This new generation included Thomas Richardson, a Quaker who moved from Boston to Newport in 1712, Daniel Ayrault, a French Huguenot, Godfrey Malbone, the shipbuilders William and John Wanton, and Abraham Redwood, another Quaker. Richardson succeeded where Peleg Sanford had failed, in opening direct commerce between Newport and London, and thus cutting out the costs of middlemen in Boston.

The main source of Newport's prosperity, however, remained the West Indies trade, with its lucrative traffic in slaves. The first recorded slave voyage out of Newport occurred in 1700 when Edwin Carter commanded a vessel carrying goods from the West Indies to Africa, where he traded them for blacks that he brought back to the Caribbean and sold for slaves. At least two other recorded voyages for that purpose also took place that year. Soon after, New England merchants discovered

the most profitable of all colonial enterprises, the so-called triangular trade. Merchant ships would buy molasses in the Indies, and bring it back to New England where it would be made into rum. Most of the liquor would then be sold locally, and the rest traded on the African coast for human chattels who would be sold either in the Indies or in the southern colonies. All parts of this transaction provided the hard currency needed to buy English goods. By the 1740s Newport merchants had won over a large portion of this commerce from Boston, and it would be one basis of Newport wealth until the Revolution. This trade put money not only into the hands of merchant shippers, but also provided profits and income for retail merchants, coopers, seamen, shipmasters, and hundreds of other Newporters involved directly or indirectly in maritime commerce.

For more than 30 years, at least 18 vessels a year owned in whole or in part by Newporters, set sail from Narragansett Bay for West Africa, carrying upwards of 1,800 hogsheads of rum and a small quantity of other provisions to be exchanged for gold dust, elephant tusks, camwood, and primarily for slaves. Ship captains normally purchased their slaves from British outposts at Cape Coast or the Dutch fort at Elmina. At times they also bought slaves from African tribal leaders who found it quite profitable to raid the interior villages and sell the captives to white traders. The slaves would then be sold in the West Indies in exchange for molasses, or in Virginia and the Carolinas for cash or tobacco. All told, this trade brought in upwards of £40,000 annually to Newport merchants, and could then be used to purchase fine goods from the Mother Country. Although Newport had more blacks than any other New England city, apparently ships engaged in the triangular trade brought few slaves home with them on the last leg of the voyage.

The demographic and economic diversity of Newport translated into politics as well. Commercial towns like

Newport often found a convergence between the economic elites and the political elites.

The town's business leaders wanted political policies that would favor commercial development, and so could not afford to stand by and leave the government to those whose interests differed from theirs. The complex nature of the Newport elite is explained in part by the fact that many of the city's business leaders were immigrants who had not arrived until the early 18th century or later. Although some, such as the Jews, could not be politically active because they were denied citizenship, they were still able to exercise political influence through their contacts. So long as Christian merchants looked after their interests, then those of the Jewish merchants would be protected as well.

Newport suffered many of the problems that afflicted other New England commercial towns in the 18th century, such as the tension between the commercial downtown and the rural surroundings. In 1741 the freeholders living in the "wood's part" petitioned the General Assembly to divide Newport into two towns. These rural folk claimed that no common bonds existed between them and the business people, and that they were "greatly injured, being obliged to bear a greater proportion of the public charge and expense of said town, than the other inhabitants, without being taken notice of." In 1743 the Assembly did in fact divide Newport, with the new rural township named Middletown.

Economic activity, of course, centered on the waterfront, with Thames, Water, and Ann Streets and the Long Wharf the main commercial arteries. By 1764 more than 60 wharves jutted out into the bay. Crowded in between the wharves were 22 distilleries which converted West Indian molasses into rum, six spermaceti candle works, several shipyards, sail lofts, and innumerable warehouses. As early as 1732 Newport counted 110 shops and stores catering to the everyday needs of the inhabitants of the town and the surrounding countryside.

The gentlemen who created this wealth did much to improve the civic landscape of the city in which they lived. In the late 1730s Newport merchants, organized as the Long Wharf Proprietors, renovated the Town

Left: Portrait of a Clergyman. Thought to be Reverend John Clarke (1609–1676), about 1659. Working closely with Roger Williams, Clarke was instrumental in negotiating and bringing back the 1663 Royal Charter for the Plantation and Colonie of Rhode Island.

Wharf that had originally been built in 1702. This not only improved the appearance of the dock area, but the larger structure could now accommodate bigger ships entering the harbor. The Town Wharf not only boasted shops and warehouses, but in the 1750s the Proprietors undertook the construction of a market house on the wharf, and engaged the architect Peter Harrison to design and build what became known as the Brick Market. Many of these same merchants joined together to organize the American colonies' first library. The Quaker merchant Abraham Redwood made the initial contribution (thus earning the naming of the library after him), and Peter Harrison designed the building in 1748. The existence of both wealth and religious diversity ensured that there would also be a host of elegant houses and churches (as well as the synagogue that Harrison also designed). Prints of Newport prior to the Revolution show a bustling seaport, beyond which are large commercial buildings, churches and mansions, with open fields in the background.

By the 1760s, Newport had developed complex trade patterns with Great Britain, the middle and southern colonies, and the West Indies. Where New York and Philadelphia, the two largest ports in the colonies, sent about one-third of their ships on European voyages, Newport sent only six percent. The two larger seaports shipped marketable products from their immediate countryside to England, while, with the exception of fish, New England had little in the way of local production that the Mother Country wanted. Newporters also sold whale oil to England, secured from the developing whaling centers along the east coast. In addition, Rhode Island manufactured potash, and also handled part of

the trade in naval stores and cotton from the southern colonies. The slave trade, however, remained Newport's single most profitable enterprise, from which it could get the hard currency needed to buy British goods.

Not all of the trade to the West Indies involved slavery; some ships bore New England products to the Caribbean, sold some of them there in exchange for local produce, and then carried the remaining cargo to England. One such voyage took place in 1773 and gives us some idea of the profits that could be made by enterprising ship owners and captains.

The ship *Nancy* had been built at a cost of £1,000 sterling, and carried a cargo worth about £2,500. An additional £1,500 could be charged to port fees in Newport, Jamaica and London; insurance; wages for its crew for the 20 months of the voyage, and commissions for its captain and agents in London, making the total amount invested in the voyage £5,000 sterling. The bulk of the original cargo sold in Jamaica for £4,500; the remainder, as well as freight picked up in Jamaica, sold for £2,100 in London, while items picked up in London sold back in Newport for £400. All told, the voyage brought in £7,000 sterling at a cost of £5,000, yielding a handsome profit of £2,000, or 40 percent on the original investment. Moreover, the captain in this instance proved able to return the *Nancy* undamaged, so that after minor refitting it could once more be sent out.

The owner of the *Nancy* was Aaron Lopez, the leading merchant of Newport, its richest inhabitant, and a Jew.

CHAPTER 2 | The Early Jewish Community in Newport

Wedding Portrait of Ferdinand of Aragon and Queen Isabella of Castile, 1469 (Pintura de Los 'Reyes Católicos' que se encuentran las dependencias reales del palacio convento de las MM) with a signed copy of the Edict of Expulsion [Alhambra Decree], 1492.

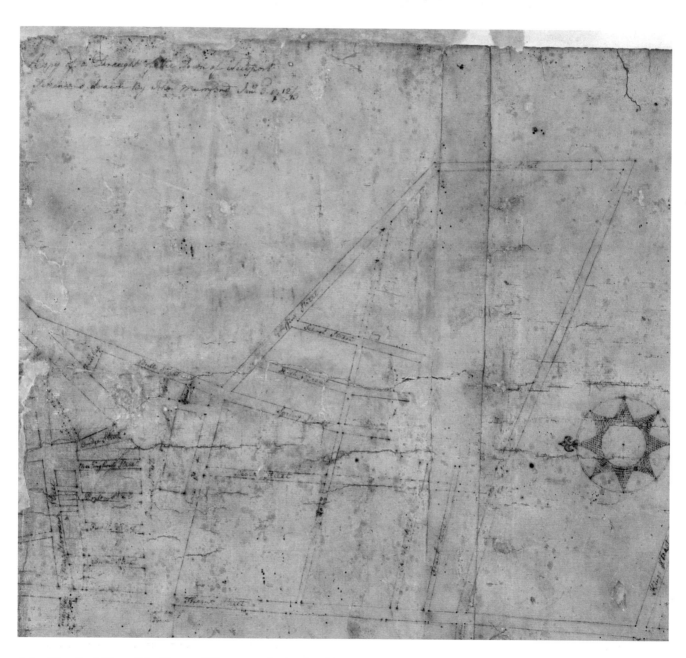

John Mumford Map of the Town of Newport, Rhode Island (1712). The map shows north on the left, east at the top. "Jew Street" (now Bellevue Ave.) is the horizontal street at the top that intersects with Griffen (now Touro) Street. The street was named because its north end started at the Jewish Cemetery created in 1677.

{ CHAPTER 2 }

The Early Jewish Community in Newport

TWENTY-THREE JEWS ARRIVED IN NEW YORK IN 1654; ANother group of Jews arrived in Newport four years later. While the Jews of New York established a community that has functioned continuously to this day, Newport's early Jewish settlers arrived in small numbers, sometimes departing and returning again for several decades before settling permanently in the mid-1700s. By the time of the American Revolution, Newport Jewry constituted a prosperous community of 25 or so families that was an integral part of the town's commercial and social life. The religious toleration and mercantile ethos of Newport meshed perfectly with the goals of Jews who came there—a desire to live free from persecution and to work hard and prosper. If this were all that happened, then the story would be like that of many other places that provided refuge; the story of Newport and its Jewry, however, is anything but typical.

Newport, as we have seen, neither preached not practiced total religious freedom; hardly any place in the world did at that time. Nonetheless, despite its nominal commitment to being a Christian commonwealth—a commitment that at times did create some unpleasantness for the town's Jewish residents—the merchants of Newport cared less about what a man believed than how well he behaved in his business dealings. In that milieu, the small Newport Jewish community did very well indeed.

The story begins as does so much of early American Jewish history, with the expulsion of the Jews from Spain in 1492, when thousands of Spanish Jews took refuge in Portugal. In 1497, however, forcible conversions made all of the Jews in Portugal into so-called "New Christians," comparable to the *conversos* of Spain—those who openly accepted baptism, although many but not all of whom continued to practice their Judaism secretly. One of these New Christians, named Gaspar da Gama, sailed with Pedro Alvares Cabral on the voyage of discovery that led to Portugal's claim over the land they called Brazil. Apparently a fair number of *conversos* were among the early Portuguese settlers of Brazil in the early years of the 16th century, and they continued to live and work there—as secret Jews—until the Dutch conquered Brazil between 1624 and 1630.

In October 1629, just before it captured Recife in the sugar-rich province of Pernambuco, Brazil, the Dutch government issued a toleration edict promising "the liberty of Spaniards, Portuguese, and natives, whether they be Roman Catholics or Jews." Their beliefs would be respected, and no one would "be permitted to… subject them to inquiries in matters of conscience." The edict sought to encourage Jews to settle in Brazil, both because the Dutch considered them politically reliable (thanks to the Jewish fear of the Inquisition) and because of their commercial competence. Although the edict had less to do with religious freedom than with making friends and ultimately profits for the West India Company, it nonetheless had its desired effect. Jews came to Recife and other Brazilian settlements and abandoned their sham Christianity, openly proclaiming their Judaism. Although the number of Jews who lived in Dutch Brazil is uncertain, it seems to have been as many as a thousand souls.

Portugal, however, wanted Recife and its riches back, and began a war against the Dutch in Brazil in 1645, with Portuguese forces conquering Recife in January 1654. During the 24 years of Dutch rule, the Jews who lived there had built a sizeable stable community. There would be no Jewish community of such size and structure again in South America until the early 19th century.

Despite the hostility of the home government toward Jews, the Portuguese conquerors signed a liberal armistice with the Dutch West India Company representatives in Brazil. Under its terms, Protestants and Jews living in Recife, nearly all of whom had been financially ruined by the war, had three months to leave, and most of them did. Lapsed New Christians as well as Calvinists had little doubt that if they stayed they would soon fall victim to the Inquisition. Most of the refugees returned to Holland, where at least they could enjoy religious toleration. But several ships did not go to Amsterdam; some went to the West Indies, some to New Amsterdam, and the passengers of at least one ship ultimately arrived in Newport (perhaps after a stop in Curaçao or Barbados).

What little the Jews of Recife may have known about Puritan New England could not have been encouraging. Despite the great interest in biblical Hebrew language and literature among the Puritans, they wanted nothing to do with living Jews, or for that matter any other group that did not share their religious beliefs. Nonetheless, it appears that in 1648 Isaac Abrahams appeared before a Boston notary to witness the sale of his vessel, *The Bride of Enchusen*, to Robert Scott and John Cooke. The following year a Solomon Franco arrived with a cargo consigned to Edward Gibbons. For reasons that are unclear, Gibbons either refused the cargo or was unable to pay for it, and Franco threatened to remain in Boston, since he did not have the means to leave. Anxious to rid themselves of this unwelcome visitor, the town government voted to grant him six shillings a week for ten weeks, during which time he had to book passage to Holland.

By the time Recife fell in 1654 there was already a tiny Jewish settlement in New Amsterdam (later New York). A small group of 23 refugees from Brazil took another ship there, where they received some support from the local community. But the hostility of New Amsterdam's governor, Peter Stuyvesant, led at least part of that group to leave and return to Jamaica sometime in 1655.

Other refugees still in the Caribbean now looked for another haven, and for the first time Newport appeared as a possibility. They would have learned that after initially prohibiting foreigners, including "Dutch, French, or of any other nation" from being accepted as a free inhabitant of any town in Rhode Island, a few months later the Rhode Island Assembly in December 1652 had reversed itself. Now "all men of whatever nation soever they may be, that are or shall bee hereafter received inhabitants within any of the Townes in this Collonie shall have equal libertie to buy, sell, or trade amongst us as well as any Englishman, any law or order to the contrary notwithstanding."

How did the Jews learn about the open attitudes of Rhode Island, as well as the famous letter Williams wrote to Providence with his analogy of the ship? Here we encounter the first version of our founding story about the arrival of Jews in Newport. The archives hold a petition from a Captain Campa Subado (also known as Campoe Sabbatha), who had been a pilot in the attack of Cromwell's fleet in Jamaica in 1655, and who may well have been a Jew. The petition, presented to the Rhode Island Assembly on October 11, 1656, asked for the return of his ship, seized by a privateer, and the court that heard the request was presided over by none other than Roger Williams. One assumes that Captain Subado retrieved his vessel, and upon returning to Jamaica informed his fellow Jews there about the possibilities of freedom from persecution in Rhode Island. According to this version of the story, 15 families from Recife boarded Captain Subado's ship, and sometime in 1658 arrived in Newport.

There did not seem to be any trouble between the Jews and town authorities, since the records of the period show no instances of Jews appearing in court or before notaries. The original group included Samuel Isaac and Judah Moses, soap boilers; Moses and Jacob James, workers in brass; Isaac Benjamin, Abraham Benjamin, Isaac Moses and Jacob Frannc or Franci. In 1677, the community enters the legal record by purchasing land for a Jewish cemetery.

There appear to have been enough Jewish male adults to form a *minyan*, the quorum necessary to conduct prayers, and they had brought with them a Torah scroll containing the Pentateuch, the five books of Moses. According to some sources this Torah came from Holland. Dr. Ezra Stiles, a Protestant minister and later president of Yale University, was a frequent visitor to the synagogue that the Jewish community built in the mid-18th century. Its rabbi and his friend, Isaac Touro, showed him a Torah scroll over 200 years old. There is still a very old Torah in the Touro Synagogue, written on leather rather than parchment, and believed to be the same scroll brought by the first settlers.

There is a second traditional story about the settlement of Jews in Newport: the famous and now lost fragment of a document, the date being partially obliterated, that reads:

> Ths ye l;0165[8] Wee mett att y House off Mordecai Campunell and after Synagog Wee gave Abm Moses the degrees of Maconrie.

The history of this fragment is a story in itself. Nathan H. Gould reported having found it in 1839 in an old chest that had belonged to a deceased relative. The Goulds, a Quaker family, had at the time a unique relationship to the Touro Synagogue—during the 19th century, after the once prosperous Jewish community quitted the city, the Goulds became the caretakers of the building. Nathan Gould showed the fragile document to the Reverend Edward Peterson, whose 1853 history of Rhode Island was for many years the standard account.

The document can no longer be authenticated, but analyses of the style and content have led some scholars to vouch for its genuineness. The problem is that it antedates the first known Masonic Lodge in Newport, St. John's Lodge No. 1, by 90 years. It also predates the creation of the first Grand Lodge in London in 1717 by nearly a half-century, and modern Masonic history dates from that point.

Nonetheless, groups of freemasons had existed since the middle ages, when their name described exactly what they did, carve the stone statues and decorations on the great cathedrals and castles rising all over Europe. By the beginning of the 17th century, membership in freemason groups was no longer limited to stone carvers,

and usually included at least one powerful member of the nobility, often a member of the royal family, to provide protection. The Grand Lodge that came into being in 1717 consolidated earlier and smaller "lodges," and so Masons clearly existed before that year. The Masons prided themselves on their liberal attitudes, and their lodges were open to anyone who believed in God, or as one document said, "the Great Architect of the Universe." This meant that not only Protestants but Catholics and Jews could join as well.

The subsequent presence and experiences of this first group of settlers are virtually undocumented in the historical record. For this reason, some scholars believe that the date of permanent Jewish settlement in Newport is later than 1658. The first surviving written record of their presence is dated 1677, the year the Jews purchased land for a burial ground. Obviously, they were already living in Newport or would not have made the purchase. Until some new archival proof of Jewish settlement in Newport appears, the traditional settlement 1658 date is likely to remain the "official" one.

The history of each early American Jewish settlement is consistent in certain respects. Jews would come into a new place, and as soon as they had sufficient numbers would gather in an informal *minyan* for the purpose of prayer. Later, if the community prospered, it would build a synagogue. The other necessary component of a Jewish community was a burial ground and the community would often seek land for its cemetery before an actual need arose. The deed for the Newport Jewish cemetery lends credence to setting the date for arrival 19 years earlier, as well as providing proof that the original group had left, and then returned a few years later, since one passage says "if it Should So fall out that yᵉ Jews Should all Depart the Island Again." One reason for this return might have been that in 1663 John Clarke succeeded in obtaining the colony's charter from England's King Charles II assuring freedom of worship and conscience. Or perhaps an easing of the Navigation Laws gave a new set of merchants a greater incentive to come to Rhode Island and join in the imperial trade.

The Jewish cemetery, still in existence, is located where Newport's now-elegant Bellevue Avenue begins at Kay Street. In the 1670s, however, this parcel consisted merely of a barren stretch of land on the outskirts of town; there appears to have been no objection raised to locating a Jewish burial ground there. Mordecai Campanall (the same who participated in the Masonic ritual) and Moses Pacheco purchased the land for the Beth Chayim—the abode of life, the traditional name for a Jewish cemetery—for the use of the "Jews and their Nation Society of Friends." The document, clearly one of the most important in Newport Jewish history, is worth quoting in full:

> *This Witnesseth that I Nathaniel Dickens of Newport in Rhode Island Cooper have sold for a Valuable Consideration in hand Received unto Mordicay Campanall & Moses Pacheicko Jews and their Nation Society of Friends a Peice of Land for a burial Place being in D(e)mentions followeth, that is to Say Peise of Land thirty foot long, Butting South West upon the Highway that Leads Down from ye Stone Mill toward Benja: Griffins Land and thirty foot upon John Eastons Land and thirty foot upon the Line North west butting upon a Slip of Land which ye Said Nathaniel Dickens hath yet Remaining betwixt this Peise of Land now Sold and ye Land Now belonging unto Benjamin Griffin and ye Line Northeast Butting also upon ye Said Nathaniel Dickens his Land to be in Length fourty foot, which Said Passell of Land in Dimansions as aforesaid with the Fences thereto Pertaining. I have for my Self my heirs and Assigns or Successors for them to Possess, and Enjoy for the Use as abovesaid forever they from henceforth Making and Maintaining Substantialy Fences Round ye Said Land but if it Should So fall out that ye Jews Should all Depart the Island Again So as that these shall be none left to keep up & Maintain the Fences as aforesaid then the Said Land shall Return Again to the said Nathaniel Dickins his heirs Executors Administrators or Assigns for him or them to Possess and Enjoy Again as freely As if no such Sale had been Made and Witness of this Sale hereof the Said Nathaniel Dickins hath hereunto set his hand and seal this 28th day of February 1677.*

> *Nathaniel Dickens His mark and seal In the presence of George Hamonde James Huling*

This relatively small piece of land was later enlarged, adding the plot which Dickens identified as still belonging to him. The Easton land is now marked by the

Easton House. Because of the location of the cemetery, the road leading from the Stone Mill became known as Jew Street—not because of Jewish residences there but because of the burial ground—and shows up on maps of Newport as early as 1704 as such. The Jews did erect a wooden fence around the Beth Chayim that lasted until 1822, the year that the last Jew in Newport, Moses Lopez, left for New York. But a few months earlier the deteriorating wooden fence had been replaced by a new brick wall, costing one thousand dollars, through the generosity of Abraham Touro, the eldest son of *Hazzan* Isaac Touro. Abraham had been born in Newport and spent his early childhood there. At the time of his contribution he was a successful merchant living in the Boston suburbs.

The burial ground in Newport is not the first Jewish cemetery in continental North America; Jews in New York secured a small plot from Peter Stuyvesant in 1656, and then bought a larger piece of land in 1682. A puzzle is that the earliest extant tombstone in the Newport cemetery dates from 1761, as contrasted with 1683 in New York. Clearly there had to have been internments between 1677 and 1761, and one can only guess at why no evidence remains of them. Perhaps the grave markers were too perishable, or they fell in as the ground subsided, a not uncommon phenomenon in old cemeteries.

Although Roger Williams proposed a Christian colony, he also wanted no persecution of minority sects. As noted earlier, he hoped to convert Jews, Papists and others to the true faith, but believed that letting them live in peace so they could learn the error of their ways would be the most efficacious method. Although the Jews who came to Newport in the latter part of the 17th century did not face the overt persecution of the Inquisition, it would be naïve to think that Protestants who had come here from England had not brought at least some antisemitism as well as a great deal of anti-Catholicism in their cultural baggage. Like Catholics, Jews could not become naturalized citizens in Rhode Island or achieve full legal status before the Revolution. Rhode Island's

Right: Touro Family Graves, Colonial Jewish Burial Ground (2008).

TO THE MEMORY OF
JUDAH TOURO
BORN, NEWPORT, R.I. JUNE 16, 1775
DIED, NEW ORLEANS, LA. JAN. 13, 1854
INTERRED HERE, JUNE 6,

colonial Jews faced some instances of overt discrimination. What is amazing is the rarity of these instances, plus the fact that in two well-known cases, the authorities protected the Jews from lawsuits generated by little more than prejudice.

Before looking at these cases, one should note several things. Jews came to Newport, as they did to other places in British North America, in small numbers—sometimes an individual, sometimes a family, and on occasion a small group of families. It was apparently easier for a single Jew or a small number of Jews who already had experience in trade to find a place in a mercantile economy.

Unlike much of Europe, where Jews had lived in ghettos since the middle ages, English officials made no attempt at residential segregation by religion once Jews were permitted back in Great Britain, and imperial officials followed this same policy not only in Newport but in the other colonies as well. According to Newport town records indicating where Jews resided in Newport in the 18th century, it is clear that no ghetto existed there. As already noted, the appellation "Jew Street" given to what is now the northern end of Bellevue Avenue, derived not from the fact that Jews lived there, but that the road ran alongside the Jewish cemetery.

In 1679 a contingent of Jews from Barbados came to Newport, possibly through the offices of Moses Pacheco, who had been in Barbados in 1672, and then five years later, along with Mordechai Campernell [Modecai Campanall], had purchased the land for the cemetery. Nearly all of these newcomers were merchants, and because of their familial connections in the West Indies, began to ply inter-colonial trade. The Navigation Acts of 1660, however, forbade foreign merchants—i.e., those not naturalized as British subjects—from engaging in this trade. In New York, after the transfer of New Amsterdam to English rule in 1664, Jews there had been granted the rights of free denizens which, while not as secure as becoming a naturalized citizen, nonetheless opened the doors of foreign trade to them. A denizen is one who is admitted by favor to part of the rights of citizenship, which he or she did not possess by virtue of their birth.

In Rhode Island, however, despite the welcome mat that had been laid out for all faiths, the laws still prevented Jews from being either naturalized or given the status of free denizens. But while the laws said one thing, practice said another. At this time Great Britain only fitfully enforced the Navigation Acts, and most Rhode Island merchants valued business over another man's religion. Jews received a mixed signal—laws stating they could not engage in trade, and a business community saying they could—so they sought some resolution. A group led by Simon Mendes and David Brown petitioned the Rhode Island General Assembly for clarification, and on the same day that it received the petition, June 24, 1684, the Assembly:

> *Voted in answer to the petition of Simon Medus, David Brown, and associates, being Jews, presented to this Assembly, bearing date June the 24th, 1684, we declare that they [the Jews] may expect as good protection here as any stranger being not of our nation residing amongst us in his Majesty's colony ought to have being obedient to his Majesty's laws.*

The statement is curious in several ways, not least because Jews were technically considered "strangers," and therefore under the laws of Rhode Island ineligible for either naturalization as citizens or free denizens. Even so, the mere fact of their being Jews, a fact that in most other colonies would have been a heavy disadvantage, did not seem to matter to the Assembly. So long as Jews obeyed the law, they would be welcome.

One also, however, has to see the swift action of the Rhode Island Assembly in the larger imperial context. Following the Restoration of 1660, King Charles II had followed a policy of salutary neglect toward the colonies; the Crown did not effectively enforce the Navigation Acts, nor did it attempt to rein in the growing autonomy of American colonial legislatures. While it would be completely misleading to say that Rhode Island was a self-governing colony in the latter part of the 17th century, in most matters it paid nominal fealty to the king, and then legislated as local concerns dictated.

In early 1684, however, the Lords of Trade in England, responsible for the governance of trade amongst the colonies and with the mother country, won an important court decision that annulled the charter of Massachusetts. If one royal charter could be negated, then so could others, including the very liberal one that Rhode Islanders enjoyed. The Rhode Island Assembly not only acted in the spirit of Roger Williams (who had died the previous year), but reasserted its authority against what it knew would be efforts by Great Britain to tighten control over its North American colonies.

Rhode Island's fears turned into reality when Charles II died and his brother, the Catholic James II, ascended the throne. The Lords of Trade had gotten nowhere in their entreaties to Charles to allow them to reorganize the colonial governments so that England would have greater and more direct control. Their proposal found favor with James's autocratic notions. James attempted to forcefully assert his royal prerogatives by approving a proposal to create a "Dominion of New England," and to place under its authority all colonies from Massachusetts south to New Jersey. Had James ruled longer, it is likely that a similar plan would have been imposed on Pennsylvania and the southern colonies.

A new royal governor, Sir Edmond Andros, appeared in Boston in 1686 to establish his jurisdiction, which he soon extended to Connecticut and Rhode Island. A soldier used to taking and giving orders, honest, efficient and loyal to the Crown, Andros totally lacked the political tact that the circumstances required. He began imposing taxes on his own authority, and the general resentment he generated might well have burst into rebellion had the experiment not been shut down by news of the Glorious Revolution of 1688, which replaced James II with the more tolerant William and Mary as English monarchs.

Even before Andros arrived in Boston, the Lords of Trade had begun implementing plans for tighter control over the colonies and greater enforcement of the revenue-generating Navigation Acts. They appointed Major William Dyer as surveyor-general of customs tax collection in all of the American colonies. With headquarters in Boston (seen by the Lords of Trade as the hub for smuggling and violations of the trade laws), Dyer had responsibility to administer the Navigation Acts, and before long he began seizing ships and imposing heavy fines.

About this time, the Crown brought charges of alienage against the Jews of London, who, as endenizened aliens, had been exempt from the penalties and fines imposed by the First Navigation Act. As such, they stood on roughly the same footing as native-born Christian merchants. The death of Charles II led the new government to dub them aliens in order to seize the Jews' property and drive them out of business, a tactic cheered on by non-Jewish London merchants. Dyer no doubt learned of this, and despite the fact that he had been associated with Roger Williams in securing the royal charter of 1663, now brought charges against the Jews of Newport as "aliens," and seized their property. The objects of his prosecution included four members of the Campanall family, Saul Brown, Abraham Burgos, Aaron Verse, and one woman, the widow of Simon Mendez, who had taken over his business. Their crime—they had, as aliens, been conducting trade closed to them by law.

On March 31, 1685, the general court met in Newport with Governor William Coddington presiding and a number of the colony's leading officials in attendance. Coddington swore in the grand jury, and then learned that Dyer, who had started the proceedings, had not appeared. He did have a proxy (an attorney) to represent him, but had failed to post the required bond for the property he had seized. With Dyer absent and unable to present his case, the defendants asked the court to enter a non-suit and dismiss the charges against them.

Coddington, however, believed that important reasons existed why the case should go on, and after he explained his reasoning to the defendants, they agreed. All of them had been living in Newport for at least seven years, and knew that their neighbors on the grand jury, even while disagreeing with their theology, had treated them fairly in business.

The results did not disappoint them. The jury found for the Jews, and Major Dyer suffered a humiliating defeat. In addition, the court ordered him to pay costs to the amount of 15 shillings, 8 pence. The defendants recovered their property, and went back to their trade.

This brief statement of the incident, about which little more exists, nonetheless invites speculation as to the actions of both Governor Coddington and Major Dyer.

The Deed

Mordecai Campanall (the same who participated in the Masonic ritual) and Moses Pacheco purchased the land for the Beth Chayim—the abode of life, the traditional name for a Jewish cemetery—for the use of the "Jews and their Nation Society of Friends."

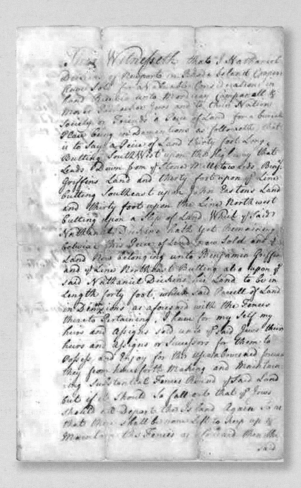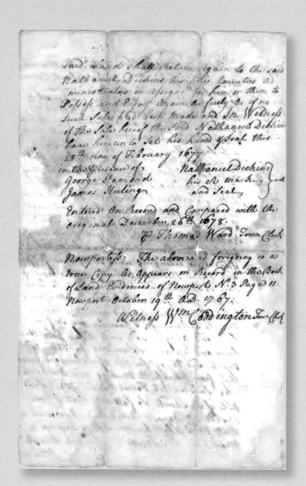

Copy of the deed for the land of the Colonial Jewish Cemetery in Newport, Rhode Island February 28, 1677/78.

Why didn't Dyer, after going to the trouble of seizing the goods of the seven Jews, appear at the trial? Why did he not take the least precaution against the results of his failure to appear—the posting of a bond? With the political scene in such turmoil due to the death of the king and the proposal for the Dominion of New England, it would have been far more discreet of the colonial governor to be more accommodating to Dyer.

We do know that little love was lost between Coddington and Dyer, and only a few months earlier Coddington had refused to turn over one Captain Paine to Dyer for trial on some charge. Although he had needed the governor's assistance—or at least his acquiescence—in seizing the defendants' goods, Dyer might well have expected that Coddington would not be a friendly or even a neutral judge at the trial. Perhaps the most important consideration to Dyer was the Assembly action of less than a year earlier, in which with little debate the legislature had said, in effect, that it cared not what the Navigation Acts said about alien traders. So long as these "aliens" obeyed the law, they would be welcome to do business in Rhode Island. In some ways, the resolution of June 24, 1684 determined the trial results of March 31, 1685.

Despite these successes, the Jews of Newport never did gain the right to naturalization. One must keep in mind that many minorities, not just Jews, found themselves deprived of what we would consider basic rights, not just in the colonies, but in the mother country from which the colonies took their lead. Some Jews had settled in England in the 12th century and acquired limited economic rights. The government eventually stripped them of all rights and Edward I expelled them from the country in 1290. Although a very small number of Jews continued to live in London during the next few centuries, Jews only began returning for more extensive settlement after the Restoration. However, they lived under the protection of the Crown, with no rights to call their own. In 1664 Jews received protection in their religious practices by Orders in Council. Eleven years later these rights were confirmed, but any religious freedom Jews enjoyed in England depended upon the generosity of the monarch, and this situation prevailed until reform legislation during Queen Victoria's reign. Gradually Jews achieved the individual rights

of Englishmen, but not until Nathaniel de Rothschild was raised to the peerage in 1885 could this process be considered complete.

Aside from political rights, however, important questions of settlement and economic liberties depended upon one's status. The first right that Jews had to fight for in the colonies was that of settlement. The issue rose initially in New Netherland in 1654, then a Dutch colony. While the founders of the Massachusetts Bay Colony envisioned a "City Upon a Hill" populated only by the faithful, the companies and proprietors of the other colonies wanted settlers. It is not that religion counted for nothing; being a Jew or a Catholic would be a disadvantage throughout the colonial era. The orders Peter Stuyvesant received from the Dutch West Indian Company, to allow the Jews to stay in New Amsterdam, were confirmed once the British took over. Other colonies saw Jewish settlers slowly arrive, and so by the latter part of the 17th century the right of settlement seems to have been won. Of course, one needs to keep in mind that the numbers involved were small indeed. This is not the great wave of immigration that came over in the millions between 1880 and 1924, or even in the tens of thousand between 1840 and 1880. We are talking of individuals, families, and in a very few instances, small groups of families.

Once allowed to stay, Jews also had to be allowed to earn their living, and rights of trade belonged to and were closely supervised by the Crown. In the British West Indies, English planters, wanting to utilize the overseas contacts of Jewish merchants, successfully petitioned the Council on Trade and Plantations (the Lords of Trade) to license some Jewish traders. The Navigation Act of 1660, however, required that goods imported into or exported out of any British colony had to be carried in English-built and English-owned ships, of which the master and three-fourths of the crew were English. This clearly barred aliens—even if they had the right to live in England or in the colonies—from engaging in the lucrative colonial trade.

Yet the importance of the Jewish networks in the colonies and with Europe made it almost imperative that some loopholes be found in this blanket prohibition. In the period prior to 1696 the records indicate that Jews did business in the plantations, either under local acts passed specifically for this purpose or under letters patent of denization.

Thus the declaration of the Rhode Island General Assembly in 1684, the failed attempt by Major Dyer a year later, and the practice of denization are all part of this larger pattern to make room within the imperial trade policy for Jews to do business.

The small but growing role of Jews in this trade can be seen when Parliament drafted the Navigation Act of 1696. In its original form, the law included a provision forbidding persons not native or born in England, Ireland, or the British possessions from engaging in trade or as a merchant or factor in any of the colonies. This would have closed the existing loopholes, and barred even those Jews who had succeeded in becoming naturalized or securing letters of denization. A group of English Jews representing themselves as "those of the Hebrew Nation residing at London," and acting "in behalf of their brethren, merchants and factors in his Majestie's Plantations," formally protested against this provision. In their letter they noted that for more than 40 years Jewish traders and planters had been "kindly entertained and mercifully protected" and had always traded "with all manner of freedom." The Jews received support from French Huguenots attempting to help their co-religionists in New York and the Carolinas. The petitions had their effect, and the final version of the law omitted the objectionable provision.

The 1696 Navigation Act, however, merely avoided the explicit exclusion of Jews and other aliens from trade; it left the status of these groups unchanged, and subject to the vagaries of local assemblies as to how they would be treated. At the time, English law did provide for naturalization of foreigners, but required that the person seeking naturalization profess a Christian belief and provide proof that he had taken the sacrament in a Protestant church. Jews clearly could not meet these conditions, and so had to settle for denization, which often proved a very costly affair and therefore available only to the wealthiest merchants.

In the colonies, however, Jews sometimes found it easier to be naturalized than in the mother country. Between

1718 and 1739, the records indicate that at least 13 Jews were naturalized in New York. Such actions may even have taken place earlier, as there is some evidence that David Brown, one of the petitioners to the Rhode Island Assembly in 1684, went to New York later that year and was naturalized. The colonies, eager to lure settlers and to take advantage of the trade networks of Jewish merchants, at all times appear to have been more lenient in their enforcement of British law on this issue than did England itself.

The Plantation Act of 1740 (also known as the Naturalization Act) recognized the needs of the colonies for settlers, and also tried to regularize the different procedures then in effect. It reduced costs, imposed a uniform seven-year residency requirement, and most important of all for the Jews, specifically exempted them from the Protestant sacrament and deleted the words "upon the true Faith of a Christian" from the oath of allegiance. Interestingly, Parliament did not make similar exemptions for Catholics, since it still considered them security risks who were plotting to put the Catholic Pretender back on the English throne. How many Jews actually took advantage of the bill is difficult to say, and according to some sources, only a small number in the mainland colonies actually became naturalized. One reason that so few Jews pursued naturalization is that it would have made little difference in their lives. As merchants, they understood that in Rhode Island and elsewhere their business connections and individual reputations mattered most, and in terms of their business lives, naturalization at that time would have little if any effect. Moreover, even if naturalized, Jews would still have no political rights; they still could not vote or hold elected or appointed office. Although technically aliens could not own land, in fact the colonies never enforced such provisions. By 1740 Jews in North America could safely assume that their real estate holdings would not be seized by the Crown on their death.

In Rhode Island, the story is somewhat complicated, with allegations that the statute books had been tampered with to prevent Jews from becoming naturalized. The primary incident involves the greatest of all the Newport Jewish merchants, Aaron Lopez who, along with Isaac Elizer, applied to the Rhode Island Superior

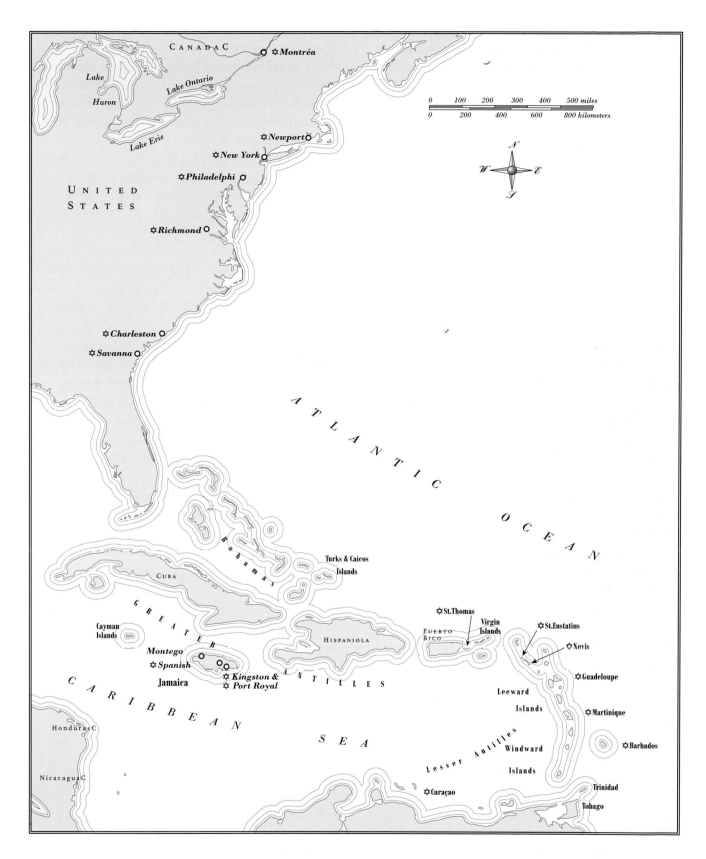

Early Jewish Communities and Congregations of North America (1620s–1790s). Prior to the establishment of these communities there is evidence of individual Jewish merchants and settlers in several areas. The marked cities (✡) and islands had a Jewish population large enough to build and sustain a synagogue and cemetery.

Court for naturalization, having met all of the requirements of the 1740 law. The Court refused to act on their petition, and Lopez and Elizer then appealed to the general Assembly for help. The upper house agreed that foreigners were entitled, under the 1740 act, to naturalization, but threw it back to the court as being its business to determine. The lower house voted against the petition on the grounds that they were Jews, and no member of that religion could play a role on voting or holding office in Rhode Island. Moreover, even if naturalized, Lopez and Elizer might "have leave to purchase Lands within this Colony" and to pass such property to their heirs, but inasmuch as they have declared themselves to be Jews, neither they "nor any other of that Religion is not Liable to be chosen into any office in this Colony nor allowed to give a Vote as a Freeman in Choosing others."

On March 11, 1762, the Superior Court under Samuel Ward heard some cases. First, it condemned a thief, Jonathan Sherman, to be hanged; directed that an "abandoned Negro" be hanged for arson; sentenced a man named Lawton to be put in the stocks for perjury; and dismissed the petition of Lopez and Elizer. Reverend Ezra Stiles, in court that day, reflected on the order of the cases in his diary, "The Jews were called to hear their almost equally mortifying sentence and Judgment: which dismissed their Petition for Naturalization." Stiles mused, "Whether this [the order of the cases] was designedly, or accidental in proceeding upon the business of the Court I dont learn."

In explaining the verdict, Judge Ward said that Parliament had passed the law for the purpose of increasing the number of inhabitants in the colonies. But Rhode Island was already overpopulated, and he noted that many people born in the colony had moved to Nova Scotia because of crowded conditions. The most humiliating part of the court's decision involved its interpretation of an alleged 1663 law that refused admission as freemen to anyone not professing the Christian religion:

> Farther by the Charter granted to this Colony it appears that the free & Quiet Enjoyment Of the Christian Religion and a desire of propogating the same were the principal Views with which this Colony was settled, & by

> a Law made & passed in the year 1663, no Person who does not profess the Christian Religion can be admitted free of this Colony. This Court, therefore, unanimously dismiss the said Petition as absolutely inconsistent with the first principles upon which the Colony was founded & a Law of the same now in full Force.

As for acts of Parliament, they would be acceptable as long as they "be not contrary and repugnant unto but, as near as may be, agreeable to the laws of this our" colony of Rhode Island.

But did the 1663 law actually say what the court claimed? Did the legislature, in fact, ever pass such a law? Some scholars have argued that the 1663 law was no more than a figment of the imagination of a 1719 committee instructed by the General Assembly to compile Rhode Island's statutes. That is the first known appearance of that "law," and subsequent compilations of the colony's laws merely copied the 1719 listing. Whether the law was a hoax or not mattered little, because during the 18th century Rhode Island courts and legislators enforced it, as in the case of Lopez and Elizer.

Lopez immediately contacted one of his Boston correspondents, Henry Lloyd, who put him in touch with a kinsman, the surveyor general of customs for Massachusetts. This official in turn spoke with the governor and the chief justice of the Bay Colony, and following their suggestions, Lopez hired a lawyer and transferred his legal residence to Swansea, just over the Rhode Island line in Massachusetts. After an interval of only five weeks, the court at Taunton, Massachusetts officially made Lopez a subject of his Majesty, George III. Elizer at first also attempted to move to Massachusetts, but then changed his mind; in July 1763 a New York court granted his request for naturalization. Other prominent Newport Jews, including Moses Levy, Moses Lopez, Jacob Rodriguez Rivera and his father Abraham Rodriguez Rivera, had obtained naturalization in New York in the 1740s. Ironically, while Rhode Island would not allow Lopez or Elizer to be naturalized within the state, it did recognize their status as naturalized citizens of the British Empire.

Whether this incident marks an increase in anti-Jewish sentiment in Newport, or is due to other considerations is difficult to tell. Lopez and Elizer may have been innocent pawns caught in a political struggle between two factions. It could hardly have been economic envy, because Lopez had not yet become the great merchant he would in the early 1770s. The Rev. Ezra Stiles claimed that many Rhode Islanders could not reconcile themselves to the generous provisions of the act. "The opposition it has met with in Rh. Island," he wrote, "forbodes that the Jews will never become incorporated with the people of America, any more than in Europe, Asia, and Africa." For all practical purposes, the 1740 Naturalization Act had no force in Rhode Island, yet this did not appear in any way to affect the status of Jews living there.

The events of 1684 and 1685, even though they turned out well for the Jews involved, apparently led to a great deal of insecurity among those then living in Newport, and some of its members began to leave in 1685. Saul Brown moved to New York, where he opened a business and acted as minister for Congregation Shearith Israel. Other members of the Brown family, as well as some of the Pachecos, also came to New York. David Campanall, one of the defendants in the Dyer suit, went to Massachusetts, and died in Ipswich in 1732, while his relative Valentine Campanel became sexton of Congregation Shearith Israel in New York, a position he later handed down to Asher Campanel. Other Jews left for the West Indies, especially Barbados, but at least some stayed, a sufficient number to care for the cemetery, carry on trade, and perhaps even have a *minyan* for prayers. Moreover, when Joseph Frazon died in Boston, his body was shipped back to Newport for burial. While there may have been Jews in Newport for the next 20 years, there does not seem to have been a significant, organized Jewish community.

The evidence for Jews remaining in Newport is at times contradictory. In 1692 a French soldier and explorer, Antoine de la Mothe, sieur de Cadillac, reported to his superiors in Paris that most of the inhabitants of Newport were either Quakers or Jews, surely an exaggeration. That dour Puritan divine, Cotton Mather, dismissed Newport as the "common receptacle of the convicts of Jerusalem," but here again it is not clear about whom he is talking. Two hundred years later the leader of the Jewish community in Curaçao, reported

that in 1693 "a party of Hebrews, about ninety in number," had left Curaçao and settled in Rhode Island, yet the only evidence for such a migration is that in 1701 a merchant named Abraham Luis, who may have been a Curaçaon Jew, lived in Newport.

The events of the latter 17th century can be seen from several different perspectives. On the one hand, Roger Williams' ideal of toleration, while never fully realized, did in fact give Jews greater freedom of conscience in Rhode Island than almost any other place in Europe or in the British Empire. One must recall that Williams intended to create a Christian commonwealth, and in this he would allow liberty of conscience so that Jews, Papists, Quakers and others would be free to recognize the error of their ways and then accept the true faith. It should not be surprising, therefore, that even in Newport there should a vestige of anti-Jewish feeling.

Newport, however, also illustrates that the older models of antisemitism had little to stand on in the New World. Part of this derived from the fact that there were so few Jews; at the time of the American Revolution, the best estimate is that some 3,000 Jews lived in all of the American colonies. The stereotypes of Jews that had been so prevalent in the Old World made little sense in the New. In the colonial environment, many different national and religious groups were forced to live and work together in close proximity and therefore had no choice but to cooperate with one another. The arguments of Jews as being of a different religion lost potency when one realized that literally dozens of religious sects and denominations existed in the colonies; nor did it make sense to identify Jews as a nation, when they clearly had nothing in common on that score with the Spanish, Dutch or British.

Some of those opposed to the Jewish presence adopted a third model of separation, declaring that Jews constituted a different race, more akin to the Indians than to that of Christian religious dissenters or other European immigrants. By trying to place Jews alongside groups whose legal status in the colonies was ambiguous at best, opponents hoped to marginalize the Jews and prevent them from assuming a fully recognized place in society. These efforts failed at the time, and reflected more a discomfort some Englishmen had with Jews rather than an overt governmental policy. But the 1684 and 1685 incidents, which foreshadowed the efforts to block naturalization eight decades later, left the Jews of Newport concerned about their continued welcome there.

Whether the second community left or nearly died out, all would soon change. Newport became a great commercial seaport in the early 18th century, and its prosperity and that of a new Jewish community there went hand in hand.

Newport Harbor, c. 1740. Fort George (later Fort Washington) in the foreground with steeples (left to right) of the Friends Meeting House, Colony (State) House, and Trinity Church.

CHAPTER 3 | A Golden Era Begins

Rhode Island's Colony House in Newport (1736).
This was the colonial and state capitol for many years. It was the center of regional political life. An elegant dinner was held here for President Washington when he visited in 1790.

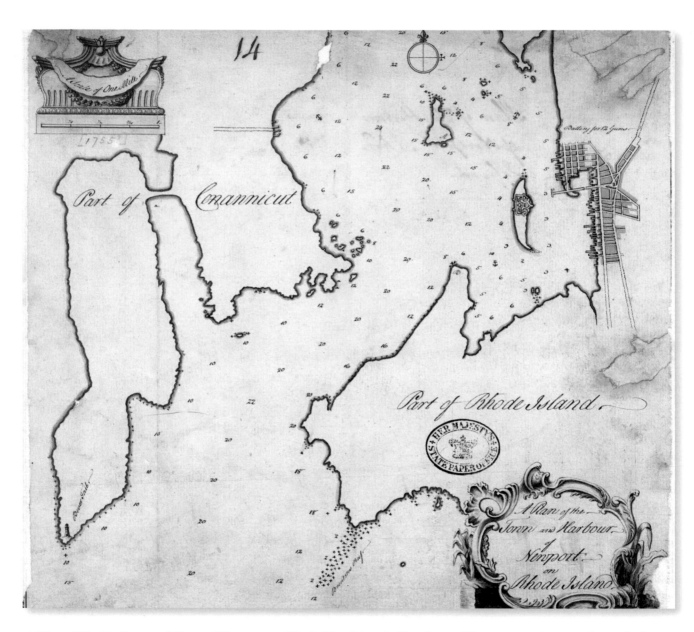

A Plan of The Harbour and Town of Newport on Rhode Island (1755). This chart of Narragansett Bay was drawn by Peter Harrison, architect of the Touro Synagogue in Newport.

{ CHAPTER 3 }

A Golden Era Begins

THE 50 OR SO YEARS BEFORE THE START OF THE AMERICAN Revolution constitute the golden era of Newport's commercial history. During that time the Rhode Island seaport accounted for a percentage of the trans-Atlantic as well as coastal and island trade well beyond its size when compared to the far larger ports of Boston, New York and Philadelphia. As Newport prospered it attracted new Jewish entrepreneurs, and in a symbiotic relationship each helped the other. Newport's growth gave Jewish merchants an unparalleled opportunity to prosper. In turn, their networks and mercantile talents contributed greatly to the growth of the small city they now called home.

Newport in the 17th century had hardly been a sleepy seaside resort, and while it economically outshone Providence, neither settlement could be considered a serious economic competitor to Boston or New York. In fact, Newport depended on those two cities for imported European goods up until the 1730s. The one area where Newport ship owners seemed to have carved out a niche was the West Indian trade. Newport also differed significantly from Providence, particularly in the diversity of its population, and in many ways this diversity contributed to its phenomenal 18th-century growth and prosperity.

When the well-known Anglo-Irish philosopher and cleric, Bishop George Berkeley, arrived in Newport in 1729, people of all sorts turned out to greet him, and he declared: "The town of Newport is the most thriving place in America for bigness." By this Berkeley meant not only economic and commercial growth, but social, religious and cultural undertakings as well. At the time one could count three Baptist churches, two Congregational, one Church of England, and a Friends meeting house. The

Jews had not yet built a synagogue, but met for services in private homes. Almost from the beginning Newport had a public school supported by taxes, and by the early 1700s there were several booksellers doing business in the town. An attempt had been made in 1705 to establish a printing press in the city, and in 1732 James Franklin, Benjamin's brother, began editing and publishing a newspaper.

Bishop Berkeley was on his way to Bermuda to start a college, and had originally intended to stay just a short while in Newport, but he was so taken by the town that he built a house and stayed for two years. He brought with him a small group of intellectuals and artists, and they too found a receptive environment. Berkeley organized a series of lectures on "Divinity, Philosophy, Morality and History," and as one contemporary reporter noted, "The Quaker, the Baptist and the firm supporter of the Church of England maintained each his part; but the Quaker preacher and the Jewish Rabbi alike tenacious of their rules and doctrine, listened respectfully to the preaching of Berkeley."

At the time of Berkeley's arrival Newport, while small, nonetheless accounted for more than a fourth of Rhode Island's population. In 1708 the census had shown 2,208 people living in Newport; by 1730 this had more than doubled to 4,640, with the colony's total 16,950. The population more than doubled again by the Revolution, and the growth resulted directly from the expansion of trade activity during the first half of the 18th century. While the slave trade, inaugurated in Newport in the 1720s, certainly played an important role in this growth, Newport ship owners dealt in many other products as well. As the Atlantic colonies thrived, coastal trade among them grew correspondingly, a great deal of it carried on Newport bottoms, including whale oil, candles, rum, and other staples of New England commerce. In 1764, of the 519 vessels that cleared customs in Newport, seven out of ten sailed to ports in the other continental colonies, and another 25 percent traded with the West Indies. For all that the slave trade played an important role in the city's commerce, it involved only one out of every 20 ships. Ship owners in many ways preferred the colonial and Caribbean trade because they could send smaller vessels, and make a high profit on the goods transported both ways.

If going out to sea constituted the most visible form of Newport's prosperity to outsiders, townspeople recognized that nearly all of the businesses that lined Newport's streets and docks depended on the ocean-going fleet. Shipwrights, caulkers, braziers, sail-makers, rope-makers and others ensured the seaworthiness of the vessels and provided the necessary provisions. The money earned on these voyages supported the artisans who made furniture, clothing, shoes, silverware, and clocks. As the city grew, houses had to be built, necessitating the services of carpenters, bricklayers, plasterers, painters and cabinet-makers. Lawyers, factors and others contributed to the primary commercial activity of Newport—sea trade.

Just as important from a business viewpoint, the political chaos that had marked Rhode Island in the 17th century finally ended. The colony's original four towns—Providence, Newport, Portsmouth and Warwick—had little in common with each other besides their dislike of Massachusetts and opposition to any form of religious coercion. As a result, each guarded its autonomy jealously, with the inevitable result of an extremely weak colonial government. Within the four townships squabbles over land allotments and religious practices were frequent. Both Massachusetts and Connecticut eyed Rhode Island's rich lands and at various times claimed parts of it. Before merchants could begin to achieve commercial eminence in external trade, the colony had to get its internal affairs in order. The colonial government had to be strong enough to pass laws effectively regulating business transactions, guarantee land titles, and create courts to enforce contracts and debt payments. The colonial government of the 17th century had been unable to do any of these.

Resolution took place in the first decades of the 18th century, thanks in large part to Samuel Cranston of Newport, who served as the colony's governor from 1698 to 1727. After a successful career as a ship captain and merchant, Cranston turned his considerable talents to politics, and with his business knowledge managed to get the wrangling factions to agree on methods of resolving land disputes and establishing the necessary institutions to promote commerce. As for religious diversity, it increased in the 18th century, while the intensity of theological disputes faded as local churches became stable institutions. The religious liberty for which the first settlers had fought had now become commonplace, and could be accepted by both old-timers as well as new immigrants. By mid-century, Jews, Huguenots, Anglicans, Quakers, Baptists, Catholics and Presbyterians all rubbed elbows in peace. People were too busy with their businesses to worry about religious differences, and despite the large number of sects, there were fewer quarrels about religion than anywhere else in the colonies.

All in all, Newport beckoned to those who would make their fortune and live free from the religious bitterness that still marked much of Europe and parts of the New World. A new generation of Jews heard the call and responded.

In 1730, New York had the only full-fledged Jewish community in what would become the United States, boasting both a synagogue and a cemetery. How many Jews lived in Newport is uncertain, and while they did not yet have a house of worship they did have a *minyan*, a quorum of ten men for prayer, and there is other evidence to mark their existence. We know that an Isaac Naphtali, his wife and son, lived there in 1695. Daniel Campanal ran afoul of the law and his misdemeanor cost him £8 15 sh. in 1700. By 1705 Jews had established a soap factory in the town, and labored as brass and iron workers in foundries. Jewish silversmiths as well as tailors could be found in these years. Moreover, although their tombstones do not exist, burials took place in the cemetery, and the clause that would have revoked the deed of land given by Nathaniel Dickens in 1677—"if it Should So fall out that ye Jews Should all Depart the Island Again So as that these shall be none left to keep up & Maintain the Fences as aforesaid then the Said

Land shall Return Again to the said Nathaniel Dickins his heirs Executors Administrators or Assigns"—was never invoked.

Numbers are a constant problem in dealing with the colonial Jewish community, since nearly all are unreliable. In 1760 the Reverend Ezra Stiles counted 15 Jewish households in Newport consisting of 58 people. Nine years later he tallied 25 families. A 1774 colonial census listed Newport with 9,209 inhabitants, but a search for every known Jewish name, as well as those that appeared to be, yielded only 121 men, women and children. At the very most, Jews accounted for no more than two percent of Newport's population, and yet a miracle seems to have happened. Long after the community had peaked in size, it kept increasing. In 1863 Governor William Cozzens declared that "some hundreds of wealthy Israelites" had moved to Newport between 1750 and 1760. An article by H. T. Tuckerman in 1869 claimed that the synagogue "boasted eleven hundred and seventy-five worshippers," a throng that only could have been accommodated in such as small building by a day-long series of successive services. Even for non-Jews, Newport Jewry has always seemed larger in size and significance than its actual numbers.

Beginning around 1740, in reality, one finds a small but constant influx of Jews into Newport that lasted for two decades. Among the names found on the town rolls during this period are Judah Israel, Solomon Hays, Isachar Polack, Tuchar Polock, Zacharia Polock, Henry Myers, Saul Abrahams, Jacob Francks, Abraham Hart, Jacob Juda, Israel Abrahams, Aaron Cardozo, Naphtali Hart, Naphtali Hart Myers, Isaac Hart and Samuel Hart, not to mention the most successful family to settle in Newport, Moses Lopez, his brother Aaron, and Aaron's father-in-law to be, Jacob Rodriguez Rivera. Although most of these names are Sephardic, Newport, like the other major Jewish communities in the colonies, also had a fair number of Ashkenazic Jews, those who came from central Europe rather than from the Iberian Peninsula. (There is evidence that ship captains sometimes transported Jewish passengers to Newport on speculation that they could collect the passage money from the philanthropy of Newport's Jews.)

The Jews who came to Newport, although small in number, nonetheless brought with them valuable assets that enabled them to succeed in the town's greatest industry, overseas trade. Chief among these may have been the extensive familial network that existed in the Sephardic community. To give one example, Moses M. Gomez, the seventh child of Mordecai Gomez, a merchant in New York, married Esther Lopez, the daughter of Aaron Lopez of Newport. Another member of the Gomez clan, Isaac Gomez Jr., married Abigail Lopez, another of Aaron's children. In the 1760s when Aaron Lopez sought to expand his trade with Jamaica, he approached Isaac Pereira Mendes, a Jamaican merchant, to serve as his commercial agent. Isaac Mendes declined, but recommended in his stead his brother Abraham, who happened to be Lopez's son-in-law. Another prominent merchant, Isaac Mendes Seixas of New York, had two sons, Moses and Abraham, who married respectively women from Newport and Charleston, while their sister married a merchant in London and a niece wed a trader in Kingston, Jamaica. A strong web of marriages bound together Jews in the Caribbean, London, Amsterdam, New York, Philadelphia, Charleston, Savannah and Newport. These ties proved invaluable, and not just for business purposes. They reminded the Sephardim who they were and from whence they had come.

Jews who had been forced to live outwardly as Christians while secretly maintaining their Jewish rituals in Spain, Portugal, or Iberian colonies in the New World shared a commonality of experiences unknown to those who had always been able to live openly as Jews, even if in terrible circumstances. Among the Sephardim, writing in Spanish or Portuguese renewed and maintained bonds of kinship, even if the correspondence related only to business matters. Isaac da Costa, a successful merchant, had lived in London for many years before emigrating to Charleston, South Carolina, where he served as a leader of the Jewish community and enjoyed the respect of other prosperous businessmen. Clearly his English was excellent, yet whenever he wrote to Aaron Lopez, who also spoke and wrote English well, the two men employed Portuguese for even minor business transactions. (While they probably used clerks in their offices, enough evidence exists of personal letters to show their command of English.) James Lucena, a *converso* who had chosen to live as a Christian after arriving in Newport from Portugal and who made great efforts to assimilate into the local society, also corresponded with Lopez and others in their native tongue long after he, too, had mastered English. For men like these, and for those with whom they transacted business across the seas, ties of kinship and heritage mattered a great deal, and the network they created gave them an advantage in building up their businesses.

The influx of Jews into Newport came partly as a result of Rhode Island offering greater economic opportunities than did New York, especially after the close of King George's War in 1748. By 1742 the Harts, the Isaackses and the Polocks had left New York and their names appeared on the tax rolls of Newport as transients and strangers, at the same time that they disappeared from the membership lists of Shearith Israel, New York's Sephardic congregation. In 1743 Moses Lopez arrived in Newport, and five years later Jacob Rodriguez Rivera came, although it appears that Rivera maintained a home in New York and traveled between the two cities for a few years before settling permanently in Newport. In 1752, Moses' half-brother Aaron arrived, directly from Portugal.

For all the names that we have who at one time or another lived in Newport, numbers continue to be imprecise. In the early 1750s a group of 72 traders protested the issue of paper money by the colony, and the list included only one Jew. As late as 1757 no *mohel* (ritual circumciser) lived in the town, a functionary critical for any Jewish community, and the oldest extant tombstone in the cemetery dates from 1761. Yet the odd record here and there seems to indicate that Jews began to play greater roles in the economic life of the community.

Privateering, for example, a legitimate enterprise at that time, found Jewish names listed as owners or co-owners of several ships. In both King George's War (1744–1748) and the French and Indian Wars (1756–1763), merchants, with the blessing of the British government, fitted out privateers and sent them after French shipping. In 1743 Moses Mendes and Abraham Pereira Musquita, along with a third, non-Jewish partner, fitted out the *New Exchange* as a privateer with

24 guns and a crew of 18. A few years later Abraham fitted out the *Defiance*, a large ship with 36 guns and a crew of 110. All in all, Newport Jews appear to have invested in over a dozen privateers, often in partnership with their co-religionists in New York and even Philadelphia. Unfortunately for the British, when the Newport-based privateers did encounter French ships carrying molasses, sugar and rum, rather than fighting, the captains—apparently acting on instructions from their owners—engaged in commerce, to the mutual profit of both. What some might have termed treason, Newporters and most other New Englanders called good business.

There seems to have been no part of Newport's business in which Jews were not involved. In 1750, Newporters could buy snuff from Moses Lopez, Jacob Rodriguez Rivera and Aaron Nunez Cardozo at "The Scotch Snuff Manufactory." Two years later the Assembly granted a license to Moses Lopez to manufacture potash, "the said Moses having procured the secret of its making from a particular friend that is not in this country." James Lucena, claiming "that he had acquired from the King's manufactory in Portugal the true method of making soap of the same kind and quality as that made in Castile, Spain" successfully petitioned the Assembly in 1761 for the privilege of setting up a manufactory, and as a further reward was made a citizen of the colony. (Lucena could be made a citizen because he chose to continue life as a Christian in the New World.) Newport Jews made soap and candles, sent ships out carrying everything from sheep to iron bars to rum, wrote insurance, borrowed and lent money, imported goods for local sale, and purchased local items for export. The very first effort at establishing a monopoly in America took place in 1761, and Jews played a leading role in it: cornering the spermaceti trade.

One by-product of the whaling industry that proved of great attraction to colonial consumers was spermaceti candles, made from the wax-like substance extracted from the head matter of the sperm whale. Good spermaceti candles burnt evenly, and did not have the rank smell of candles made from tallow or other animal fats. The demand proved so great that the whalers found themselves in the enviable position of disposing of the spermaceti in a sellers' market. In an effort to control the costs, nine of the leading candle makers in Rhode Island and Boston signed an agreement on November 5, 1761, establishing the United Company of Spermaceti Chandlers. In the agreement they set a maximum price they would pay for the raw material, arranged for a policing mechanism, and went so far as to promise that if on the open market the price rose to more than six pounds sterling per ton, they would fit out 12 vessels as whalers to secure the head matter for the combine at a reasonable price The signers included Jacob Rodriguez Rivera (in partnership with a non-Jew, Henry Collins), Naphtali, Samuel, Abram and Isaac Hart, and Aaron Lopez.

Apparently the agreement failed to work, because less than nine months later some of the members began to complain that others had violated the trust agreement by purchasing head matter at prices above the consortium agreement. They complained to Richard Cranch of Boston, who had led the way in creating the trust, that "we have certain information that most of the Factors at Nantucket have procur'd all the Head Matt'r they possibly cou'd, at an advanc'd price…This is a manifest Breach of the Articles." Despite the problems, the candle-makers renewed their agreement in April 1763, and apparently renewed it one year later. The market forced them to raise the maximum price they agreed to pay to ten pounds sterling per ton. While the group had not carried out their threat to enter the whaling fleet, apparently some of the signatories to the new agreement had done so on their own. What is most interesting about the new agreement is that it also divides up the head matter and assigns each of the members a certain percentage of the raw material. Nicholas Brown & Co. received 20 barrels out of every 100, Joseph Palmer & Co. 14, and Thomas Robinson & Co. 13. The importance of the Jewish members, and an indication of their manufacturing capacity, is that Aaron Lopez and Jacob Rodriguez Rivera & Co. each received 11 percent of the head matter, Naphtali Hart & Co. nine percent, and Moses Lopez two percent. Thus the Jewish members of Newport controlled roughly one-third of the spermaceti candle-making capacity in the country at the time.

The new agreement apparently did not work any better than the old one, but spermaceti candles would be a major product carried by merchant ships in the colonial and Caribbean trade throughout the 1760s. During this time invoices for candles appeared regularly on manifests for coast wise vessels to Boston, New York, Philadelphia and Charleston. In the month of February 1763 alone, Lopez sold over 3,000 £ (local non-sterling) worth of candles.

Although there are several Jewish merchants who did well in Newport's golden era, one name stands out above all others. To some extent we know more about him because he left a greater record in terms of personal papers, although most of them relate to business rather than personal or communal affairs. But contemporaries like the Rev. Ezra Stiles also considered Aaron Lopez such a unique person that we learn much about him from their comments. Scholars of Rhode Island commerce in the 18th century find his presence everywhere, from retail sales to spermaceti candles to coastal shipping to manufacturing to the slave trade. Just as Newport Jewry, despite its small size, played such a large role in the city's commercial growth, so Aaron Lopez led the way in nearly every venture he attempted.

In Portugal in 1731, the second wife of Dom Diego Jose Lopez presented him with a son, whom they named Duarte. Although it appeared that the Lopez family faithfully followed the rituals of the Holy Catholic Church, in fact they, like many *conversos*, secretly practiced Judaism. Such *conversos* could never escape the watchful eye of the Inquisition, and Dom Diego's eldest son by his first wife, named José, fell under suspicion of Judaizing, secretly practicing his true faith . Rather than be caught and face the terrors of the Inquisition, José escaped to America, where he took the name Moses, and after a short stay in New York, where he became one of the first Jews naturalized under the Act of 1740, he made his way to Newport. When he actually arrived there is uncertain; he was acting as an interpreter for the Vice-Admiralty Court at Newport as early as 1743, although he may not have moved his residence there until 1748 or 1750. Another son soon afterwards left for Jamaica, and, openly reclaiming his faith, took the name Abraham.

Duarte recognized that he, too, must be under surveillance, but gave the authorities no cause to arrest him. He married a niece, Anna. They had their first child

He was a merchant of eminence, Of polite and amiable manners. Hospitality, liberality, and benevolence Were his true characteristics An ornament and valuable pillar to The Jewish society, of which he was a member. His knowledge in commerce was unbounded and his integrity irreproachable; thus he lived and died, much regretted, esteemed and loved by all.

—Epitaph from the gravestone of Aaron Lopez

baptized as Catherine. Making his plans carefully, he arrived in America in 1752, and in October that year joined his half-brother Moses in Newport. Duarte and his family now openly confessed their Judaism, and we learn that both Duarte and his younger brother Gabriel, submitted themselves to the rite of circumcision—*el sangre del fermamento*—the blood of the covenant. He changed his name to Aaron (perhaps because of the biblical identification of Aaron as the brother of Moses), and he and Anna, now known as Abigail, remarried in a Jewish ceremony. They renamed their daughter Sarah.

There is something altogether amazing about the faith of the *conversos*, how under dire circumstances they lived outwardly as Christians yet secretly clung to Judaism, passing down its teachings and practices from one generation to another over more than two centuries. Then when they could live freely, they took up their Judaism openly and proudly.

After their arrival in Newport, Abigail bore Aaron six more children. She died, however, at the age of 36 in 1762, and none of their children reached adulthood. A year after her death he married Sarah Rivera, the daughter of Jacob Rodriguez Rivera. From this union would come ten children, two of whom were named Jacob, as well as a strong business partnership between Aaron and his father-in-law.

Lopez also kept in mind his remaining relatives in Portugal. In 1762, as the Newport congregation gathered for Day of Atonement services, the members had offered up prayers "for all our brethren held by the Inquisition and who are captives." In April 1767, Lopez had one of his captains, Jeremiah Osborne, sail from London to Lisbon before heading back across the Atlantic to Newport. In a letter received from Osborne, Lopez learned that "your friend out of the country wrote…respecting a passage to your place. We shall endeavor to conduct that affair with discretion." A few weeks later, Osborne wrote again, that they were about

ready to sail, and were merely awaiting news of the friend from out of the country, who it turned out to be Aaron's half-brother Miguel, his wife Joana, and their three sons, Duarte, José, and João. Their escape provided Aaron not only with relief regarding their lives, but also a measure of consolation for the death of his brother Moses, who had led him to the New World.

Lopez had brought little cash with him, and he set himself up initially as a small trader, in some form of partnership with his half-brother Moses. He appears to have already been proficient in English, probably having learned it from a tutor in Lisbon. He had been raised as a gentleman, and he and his wife had the social manners necessary for success in polite society. Perhaps most important, Aaron had an analytical mind which allowed him to see what he had to do to succeed at a time of great commercial expansion in Newport. He utilized his brother's connections in the New York Jewish community; among his earliest contacts were the wealthy Daniel Gomez and Hayman Levy, a successful merchant with important connections. He bought local items on short-term credit, and then sold quickly, reinvesting his profits in additional goods.

Early on he saw the value of the spermaceti trade, and within a year after settling in Newport was urging contacts in New York to take additional consignments of candles from him. When told that candles might be hard to sell, he wrote that "you must Consider I am a beginner, my Stock but small & unless I Contrive to Keep my Little Trade in a Continual Circulation it Can't answer the End of my Labours." Lopez realized that as a small merchant, he had to keep his stock moving. When the demand for tea went up, he borrowed money in order to buy additional supplies to sell.

As his business expanded, Lopez implemented certain ideas that in the end would make him the richest man in Newport. First, he needed to have credit available to him so that he could buy on a moment's notice; initially he found this credit among Hayman Levy and others whom he came to know in the New York Jewish community. Second, in many transactions, he in essence bartered one type of good for another. He might trade some of his spermaceti candles for iron or lumber, and then trade that for other commodities, in the end

Left: Aaron Lopez (1731–1782). Grand merchant prince of Newport and one of the founders of Congregation Jeshuat Israel. Several of his gifts to the synagogue community still hang in the historic building.

selling the last trade for cash and a profit. This meant that unlike some merchants, Lopez did not specialize in just candles or wood or even slaves; he bought and sold everything ranging from livestock to manufactured goods.

These steps allowed his enterprise to grow, and within a few years Lopez became one of the more successful local merchants in Newport. Lopez recognized, however, that far greater profits could be had in the colonial and Caribbean, and then eventually the trans-Atlantic, trade. But what should be sent? If his vessels carried lumber, for example, and arrived in a port where three other ships had already unloaded lumber, few if any sales would take place. So he hit upon the idea of having agents in all of the major ports where he planned to do business. These agents, by carefully watching local trends, could inform Lopez of what goods the market wanted, and at the same time find and purchase goods that Lopez wanted to import into Rhode Island. In fact Lopez used the same system in the colony itself; by 1758 he had created a trading network of agents in Coventry, Kingstown, Warwick and Cranston who supplied him with axes, pig iron and turkeys in return for tea and other goods which previously had only been available from Boston. A careful, indeed a conservative man in many ways, Lopez made mistakes in business, but rarely the same one twice.

Lopez arrived in Newport at an opportune moment, when the growing wealth of the American colonies led to greater demand for consumer goods, both the finer products made in England and less exotic merchandise as well. Consumers on the American side of the Atlantic were willing to pay for quality goods, and merchants like Lopez, who could secure these products, made a handsome profit on their resale. He and others in Newport imported and sold to the general public what had hitherto been restricted to the upper classes—quality textiles, china, metalware, wines, sugar, tea, chocolate and coffee. In addition, they manufactured goods that soon found a ready market, such as spermaceti candles. The snuff mill set up by Lopez's brother and father-in-law shipped its product to shopkeepers in New York and peddlers who sold it as far south as Virginia.

One incident is illustrative both of Lopez's manner of doing business and the difference that existed between Newport and other parts of the Atlantic market. In October 1766, Lopez sought to extend his network into Jamaica, where he proposed that a local agent would take a consignment of goods, sell them, and then either remit the cash back through a letter of credit or purchase other items that could be sold in New England. He asked Abraham Lopez Pereira, a merchant and planter of whom he had received good reports, if he would be willing to take on this business. Lopez Pereira turned him down, informing him that the system that worked so well in Newport and New York would not work in Jamaica, where planters as a rule bought on credit and thought nothing of taking years to pay off the balance. Reading between the lines of the correspondence, Pereira informed Aaron Lopez not only of the difference between the Rhode Island and Jamaica markets; he told him, in effect, that the Newporter's proposal would not work because Jewish merchants did not hold the same place in Jamaican society that they did in Newport. Lopez, a Jew, could expect fair dealings from other Newport merchants who knew and respected him, whereas the Anglo-Jamaican planter elite looked down on local Jewish merchants as "villainous men" out only to enrich themselves.

Over the years Lopez prospered mightily. He owned a fleet of ships that plied the coastal and Caribbean trades, traveled to London, and, of course, Africa. But the heart of Lopez's prosperity always remained the West Indian trade. He built up his wholesale and retail trade, and constructed a large, three-story warehouse on Lopez Wharf. On the first floor he stored goods, while he used the second for his own office and those of the various clerks he hired. The third story, extending over 200 feet in length, he utilized as a loft to make sails for his ships. Reputed to have owned the most ships in Newport, records confirm that he owned

Right: Sarah Rodrigues de Rivera Lopez (1747–1840) and her son Joshua Lopez (1768–1845), about 1775. Second wife of Aaron Lopez. Sarah lived well into the 19th century and served for many years as a matriarch for the Newport Jewish community, even after her husband's unfortunate death in 1782.

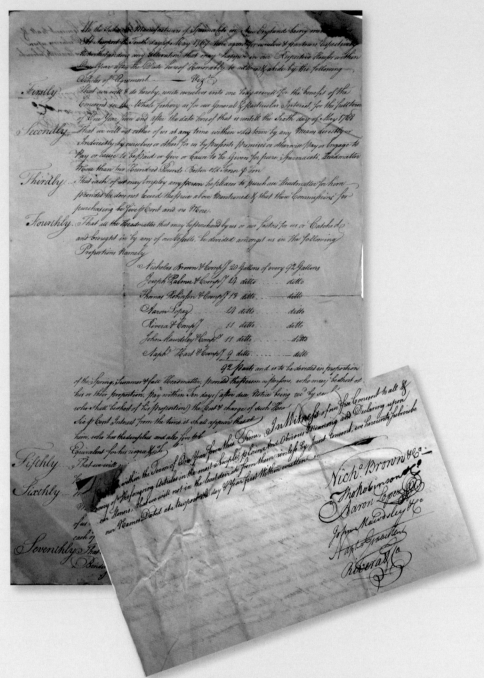

United Company of Spermaceti Chandlers Agreement

The importance of the Jewish members, and an indication of their manufacturing capacity as specified in these regular agreements was:

April 1763—Aaron Lopez and Jacob Rodriguez Rivera & Co. each received 11 percent of the head matter, Naphtali Hart & Co. nine percent, and Moses Lopez two percent; and in,

May 1767—[the agreement shown] from every 92 gallons of the head matter (spermaceti), Aaron Lopez received 15 percent, Jacob Rodriguez Rivera & Co. received 12 percent, and Naphtali Hart & Co. 10 percent.

Thus the Jewish members of Newport controlled one-third, or more, of the spermaceti candle-making capacity in the country at this time.

outright 39 vessels, and may have been part-owner of an equal number.

Although he eventually could afford to pay for most of what he personally wanted, Lopez never forgot the value of barter. In February 1772 he had built a substantial house, 36 feet across the front, two stories high, with a finished cellar and various improvements, for 809 Spanish silver dollars. The builder, Charles Spooner, gladly accepted in place of the cash its equivalent in spermaceti candles and English goods. Like many merchants, Lopez lived near his business at 131–133 Thames Street, with the buildings on the lot extending to the water.

By 1772, Aaron Lopez, who had arrived in the colony a little less than two decades earlier, had become the richest man in Newport. The tax rolls for that year of residents assessed £2 in taxes or more show Aaron Lopez at the top of the list with £37 11s., twice the amount of the two men in second place, Joseph and William Wanton. Also on the list were Jacob Rodriguez Rivera (£13 11s.), Moses Levy (£8 9s.), the Hart brothers (£5 2s.), Joseph Jacob (£4 15s.), Samuel and Moses Hart (£3 8s.), and Hyman and Simeon Levy (£2 1s.)

Both contemporary as well historical accounts of Lopez, however, speak of far more than his business acumen and his wealth. He was trusted by his creditors in a manner unique at the time. He owed the English merchant thousands of pounds sterling, and had some trouble paying the debt on time. Yet, when Cruger came to the colonies to collect from his other debtors, he went to Newport merely to have "an amicable shake by the hand…and to drink a bottle of wine with my friend, Mr. Lopez." In a similar case, Lopez owed George Hayley, a London merchant, more than £12,000 in 1774, but Hayley offered him even more credit, "since I have not the least apprehension of the whole being safe." By the following year Lopez owed Hayley £22,600, a staggering sum in pre-war colonial life, yet Hayley still had no worries. Cruger and Hayley knew that Lopez would honor all of his obligations, a fact apparently known throughout the trans-Atlantic world of commerce.

Lopez's agents appear to have been treated as colleagues as well as employees. The correspondence between

Lopez and Captain Benjamin Wright, who commanded Lopez's ship *America*, is full of bantering between the two men, and while neither ever lost sight of their proper role, there are clear indications of mutual respect between them. Henry Cruger realized that one of Lopez's ships had put into port and that no insurance had been taken out by Lopez. He immediately wrote that he himself had secured a policy, since he could not believe that Lopez would want his ships sailing without insurance.

Lopez, as some scholars have suggested, never forgot that he was a Portuguese gentleman. As such, he lived by a code of honor that required honesty in his dealings with his fellow merchants and competitors, as well as the obligation to look after the less fortunate. Jews and Christians alike appealed to him for aid, and were rarely disappointed. In a poem penned shortly after Lopez's death, Esther Freebody wrote "He was a friend, and father to the poor…In all transactions, he was just and fair."

In religious matters, Lopez strictly observed Jewish laws and traditions. He kept his places of business closed on Saturday, in accordance with Jewish law, but also on Sunday, out of regard for the sentiments of Christians among whom he lived. None of his vessels, according to some reports, ever left Newport harbor on the Sabbath. When the Lopez family had to move to Massachusetts during the British occupation of Newport, they made arrangements for kosher beef to be shipped to them on as regular a basis as possible.

Lopez employed hundreds of seamen aboard his ships, and those who left wives behind in Newport usually made arrangements for advances against the wages to be paid to the women. Seafaring in those days had little of the regularity of modern ocean crossings, and most ventures could be expected to last several months. Bad weather, or delays in selling goods in overseas ports, might extend the voyage even longer, leaving the wives with little money for food and necessities. Martha Makloud found herself "in great Want," and appealed to Lopez for money and food, hoping that her husband had "wages a nuff Due" to provide her with something. Mrs. Makloud was hardly alone. Lydia Bissell spoke for herself, and for many women married to Lopez's sailors, when she told him that "all my Dependance is upon you." Lopez apparently rarely turned down such a request for help.

One should not get the impression that every Jew who moved to Newport did as well as Lopez, or even that they all prospered. In the recession of the early 1770s Lopez got by with the help of friendly creditors. Others did not do as well, and by 1772 several prominent Jewish merchants had failed. Moses Michael Hays and Myer Polock filed for insolvency in September 1771, and Hays opened a small bookshop after release from debtors prison. Isaac Elizer petitioned for insolvency in December 1771, as did Naphtali and Isaac Hart. The tax list for 1772 showed few Jewish entrepreneurs prospering.

Lopez's father-in-law, Jacob Rodriguez Rivera, also ran into difficulty, and a series of losses forced him to stop payments to his creditors. They had such confidence and trust in him that they offered to advance him a great supply of goods so he could continue with his business, but in order to avail himself of this offer, he had to petition the Assembly for insolvency. As economic conditions improved, Rivera recovered his fortune, and a few years later—or so the story goes—invited all of his creditors in America to join him for dinner. At the table each one found on his plate payment for the full amount due to him, principal and interest.

With the outbreak of the Revolution in 1776, Lopez's business, like that of most Newport merchants, quickly deteriorated, although on the eve of the war he managed to secure permission from the British to allow his whaling fleet to set sail. Initially torn between the cause of the Crown and that of the patriots, Lopez at first did business with both sides. He removed his family from Newport before the British occupied the city, and moved to Leicester, Massachusetts, where he set up a retail shop and a modest commodities trade via overland routes to Salem, Boston, and Providence. During the war he decided to cast his lot with the patriots, and helped to supply American forces with such items as flour and leather breeches. On May 28, 1782, while returning with his family to Newport, the entourage stopped at Scott's Pond in Smithfield, Rhode Island, to water the horses. His horse suddenly plunged into deep

water and began to thrash. Lopez jumped in to try to save the horse, and in full view of his family drowned in the effort. When news of Lopez's death reached Ezra Stiles in New Haven, he wrote the following in his diary, as good an indication as any of how respected Lopez had been in pre-war Newport:

> *On the 28th of May died that amiable, benevolent, most hospitable & very respectable Gentleman, Mr. Aaron Lopez Merchant. . . .He was a Jew by Nation, came from Spain or Portugal about 1754 & settled at Rh. Isld. He was a Merchant of the first Eminence; for Honor and Extent of Commerce probably surpassed by no Mercht in America. He did Business with the greatest Ease & Clearness— always carried about with him a Sweetness of Behav. a calm Urbanity an agreeable & unaffected Politeness of manners. Without a single Enemy & the most universally beloved by an extensive Acquaintance of any man I ever knew. His Beneficence to his Famy connexions, to his Nation & to all the World is almost without a Parallel. He was my intimate Friend & Acquaintance! . . . the Demonstration of universal Sorrow attended the Funeral.*

One cannot deal with Aaron Lopez, Newport Jewry or Newport itself in the 18th century without examining their involvement in the slave trade. The sale of humans into bondage today seems so clear a violation of morality that we can barely understand how they could engage in the so-called "Guinea trade." For Jews especially, who every year at the Passover feast recall that they were slaves unto Pharoah in Egypt, the commerce seems especially appalling. But we cannot judge the 18th century by the standards of the 21st. Slavery had been an accepted part of nearly all societies since the earliest days of recorded history. Those who lost in a war expected to be enslaved, since that was the traditional fate of the losers. Even Roger Williams, who opposed "man stealing" to secure slaves, nonetheless had been involved in the sale of Narragansett captives after King Philip's War. Massachusetts Bay, it should be noted, and not Virginia, had been the first British colony in North America to adopt a law establishing permanent slavery for whites, native Americans and Africans in 1641. Providence Plantation at Williams's urging set a time limit for bondage, so that slavery would resemble something more akin to indentured servitude, but that law fell into disuse.

About the only group in colonial times to oppose slavery were the Quakers; they issued the first antislavery document in America, the Germantown protest of 1688, and began seriously to oppose involuntary servitude around 1730. At the time most other colonists considered the Quakers eccentric and extreme, and even Williams looked upon them as heretics. But no anti-slavery movement developed in Rhode Island until just before the Revolution, and not until June 1774 did the General Assembly prohibit the further importation of slaves into the colony. Immediately after the Revolution, the new state legislature passed an emancipation act in 1784, and three years later made it illegal for any Rhode Islander to be involved in the African slave trade anywhere. The law, however, appears to have been ignored by many Rhode Island merchants until 1808, when federal law prohibited the importation of any more slaves from Africa.

Rhode Island shipowners apparently began their involvement in the slave trade in the 1720s, and it continued unabated until the Revolution. As noted earlier, slavery constituted part of the "notorious triangle" of molasses, rum and slaves that laid the basis for many New England fortunes. West Indies sugar, converted into the more easily transportable form of molasses, would be carried to Newport and other New England cities where it would be converted into rum. Casks of rum would then be taken to the coast of Africa and traded for slaves, who would then be brought to the West Indies or at times to southern ports and sold for the cash needed to buy more molasses, as well as pay for British-made goods. The trade proved enormously profitable, and demanding. It required the construction of special ships to carry the human cargo, essentially floating prisons that were good for little else. In 1774 two prospective English buyers of a brig belonging to Aaron Lopez noted that it was "constructed in the manner usual for the trade from Rhode Island to Africa [and] would by no means suit for the trade from Liverpool." They meant in effect that it was too small a ship for the slave trade conducted from England, at that time the world's largest participant in the slave trade. Moreover, even though Rhode Island had the second largest rum distilling capacity in the colonies (there were 22 distilleries in Newport alone), its merchants often had to buy from Massachusetts and other places to keep up with

the demand. (Ironically, the shortage existed because Rhode Islanders consumed 48 percent of what they distilled, and sold much of the rest to buyers from Nova Scotia to Georgia. The competition existed for the ten percent that actually went into the slave trade.)

The slave trade involved high risks, and that made it quite lucrative. Slaves occasionally revolted and took over a ship. Exposure to the white man and his diseases often killed the African captives. In 1765 a ship owned by the Brown brothers lost 109 out of 165 slaves on board to sickness. Captain William English wrote to his employers, Jacob and Aaron Lopez, that he could trade "two hundred gallons [of rum] for men and 180 for women." The rum cost 18 to 25 cents a gallon to make, while slaves could bring between $250 and $400 in Havana, Charleston or Newport. Although Rhode Island was not the primary choice for slave cargoes, the colony did have a high percentage of slaves. In 1760 15 percent of Newport's population was black, yet this was not as high as in the so-called "South County," the southwestern part of the state where large sheep and dairy farms employed slaves on a plantation basis.

Aaron Lopez and other Jewish merchants did not dominate the slave trade by any means, but they did take part in it. In an age when slavery was an accepted part of commercial life, they treated it as did their contemporaries, as a business, and a profitable business it could be. No merchant dealt only with slaves; all of them bought and sold many items, usually several on any given voyage. One of Lopez's agents advised sending "Seven or Eight Hundred Barrels of Shads" to the consignee of a slave cargo, "that the Bitter and the Sweet may go together." Although not all slaving voyages proved profitable most did. Lopez's insurers talked of "the great success which the African vessels have had," and most ship owners could expect to clear anywhere between £500 and £2000 sterling per voyage. The Champlin firm averaged a return of nearly £1000 sterling a voyage between 1769 and 1775.

In most of the African voyages, Lopez partnered with his father-in-law, Jacob Rodriguez Rivera, who had probably introduced him to the trade. Rivera apparently owned interests in other vessels bound for Africa. On the whole, it appears that Lopez and Rivera sent out an average of two ships a year to Africa, a relatively small part of Lopez's overall business. Despite the high profits involved, and Lopez could gamble at times when circumstances warranted it, he apparently preferred the less risky but still profitable trade with the islands, which made up the bulk of his business. There is some evidence that Lopez wanted to increase his activity in the "Guinea trade," but could not devise a workable scheme similar to that of his other businesses, due in part to the volatility of the market.

Compared to the role of Great Britain, Portugal and France, the role of Newport in the slave trade could at best be considered minimal. At a time when Rhode Islanders transported about 106,000 slaves, ships operating out of England carried 2.5 million. Portugal, which had started earlier and persisted longer, brought even more than Great Britain. During the great wars for empire between France and England from the 1740s to the 1760s, the African voyage became extremely risky, and many Newport ship owners preferred to outfit their boats as privateers. During King George's War, for example, the colony issued privateering commissions to 35 Newport ship owners, and a third of Newport's adult males, including slaves, served on the privateers for some period or another.

For most Rhode Island merchants, the slave trade was never more than a marginal enterprise, nor was it the basis of Rhode Island fortunes. In the 18th century slaving voyages constituted only three to ten percent of ship clearances in Rhode Island each year; rarely did any merchant devote more than a tenth of his voyages to slaving. Although prominent merchants like John Brown, Aaron Lopez and Jacob Rivera and others all took part in the trade, their involvement constituted only one part of a large and complex pattern of trans-Atlantic enterprise.

A Hessian soldier who came to Newport in 1778 when the British occupied the city during the Revolution noted with astonishment that the Jewish people of the town did not differ in dress or appearance from the rest of the population. In the portraits that Gilbert Stuart painted of the Lopez family (Aaron was an early patron), we see men and women in colonial dress appropriate to an upper class household. They belonged

to this class, and despite the refusal of Rhode Island authorities to grant them naturalization or political rights, it is clear that Aaron Lopez, Jacob Rodriguez Rivera, the Harts and others were for the most part accepted in the merchant class. They achieved this status, however, not in the usual way of working up from the inside, making the right connections at school or through marriage and kinship, but by coming in from the outside and gaining recognition for their abilities and for the benefits they could bring to the market.

This seems to have been a pattern in Newport. While old family connections did count, Newport concerned itself primarily with business, and over the years the upper classes seemed to have assimilated new groups as they made their mark. Abraham Redwood (not a Jew) moved to the port from Antigua, made his fortune, was accepted into upper class society, and eventually gave the town the library named after him. The Ayrault family, Huguenots, fled from hostile neighbors in Connecticut, made money, converted to Anglicanism, and fit right in. The Wantons and Henry Collins made headway through a combination of brains, taste and political savvy. Toward the end of the colonial era, Jews like Aaron and Moses Lopez and Jacob Rodriguez Rivera began to mingle socially with the Newport elite.

It would be false to claim that no prejudice against Jews existed. Certainly the denial of naturalization to Lopez and Elizer smacked strongly of such prejudice, especially in the Assembly's condemnation of Jews as perpetual aliens. In fact, throughout the colonial period Rhode Island denied Jews and Catholics political rights, a fact that privately must have rankled these successful businessmen. Yet compared to the persecution they faced in Europe, where in many countries Jews could not pursue most professions, the inability to vote seemed a small price to pay. Rhode Island, it should be noted, not only excluded Jews, Catholics, women and blacks from the rolls but also poor and lower middle class

Right: Jacob Rodrigues de Rivera (1717–1789), about 1775. Born in Portugal, he arrived in Newport in 1748 from Curaçao. As parnas of Congregation Yeshuat Israel he was one of the three purchasers of the land for the synagogue. His daughter Sarah married merchant Aaron Lopez as his second wife.

white males. Approximately the upper ten to 15 percent of the population controlled Newport politics, hardly a participatory democracy even by 18th century standards. But this situation did not, as happened in other colonies, produce political tension. Successful Jews like Lopez and Rivera understood that their commercial interests and those of their Christian counterparts were the same, and so long as the crowd that controlled political offices did not attempt to interfere with the market, what else they did mattered little. In fact, one of the best things that happened to Newport business occurred when Samuel Cranston became governor, and introduced the reforms that made the golden age of Newport possible.

Although several Jews had been accepted as subscribers to the Redwood Library, they may—or may not—have been excluded from the Artillery Company because of their faith. In any event, in 1761 nine men—Moses Lopez, Isaac Polock, Jacob Isaacs, Abraham Sarzedas, Naphtali Hart, Moses Levy, Issachar Polock, Naphtali Hart Jr., and Jacob Rodriguez Rivera—founded a social club of their own, with rules about privileges, drinking, dinner, and the playing of cards. One name clearly absent was that of Aaron Lopez, although his brother and future father-in-law belonged. By then Lopez surely had the money to join, but perhaps he did not care for

the gaming that oftentimes seemed to be the raison d'etre for men's clubs at the time.

Aside from the Artillery Company, there seems to have been little overt discrimination against Jews, and certainly no residential segregation. By the middle of the 18th century, when the Jewish community of Newport was at its peak, Moses Lopez lived in a large house on Marlborough Street between the homes of Capt. Solomon Townsend and John Fryer. Lopez apparently did not own the house, but rented it from Col. Joseph Wanton. Moses Levy lived next to Jonathan Thurston, while the Isaacks brothers, Jacob and Moses, lived next to the wealthy Capt. John Collins.

Like many port towns, Newport did not grow by design, and it would not be until later in its development that certain sections of town became designated for the prosperous. What an amazing sense of acceptance Newport Jewry must have had. Even if they could not vote or hold office, they went unhindered in their religious practices, did not have to live in a ghetto or wear identifying badges on their clothing, and could go about their business—literally and figuratively—unhindered. The community had prospered to the point where its members could finally realize a long-held dream— to build a synagogue in Newport.

4
CHAPTER | The Sanctuary of Yeshuat Israel

Touro Synagogue, 1865.

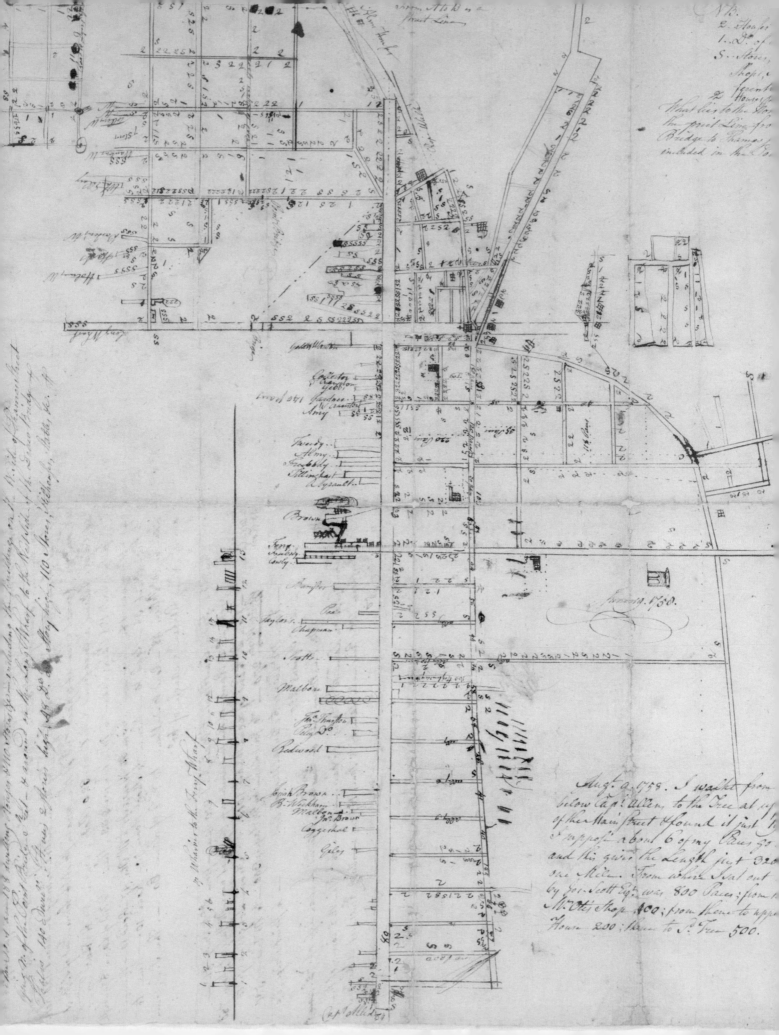

{ CHAPTER 4 }

The Sanctuary of Yeshuat Israel

FROM AT LEAST THE 1730S ON, JEWS LIVING IN NEWPORT met for religious services either in someone's home, or perhaps rented a small building somewhere. They did not have a rabbi, but may have owned one scroll of the Torah, the five books of Moses. As the community grew, the Jews of Newport realized that they needed a synagogue, a house of worship and meeting place of their own, just as the other faiths had. As they married and had families, they also needed a place that would allow them to fulfill the biblical command to teach the word of God to their children.

Synagogues, or houses of prayer and study, are as old as the Temple of Jerusalem, the seat of the high priest and the only locale where animal sacrifices could be performed. Although the ancient Israelites had an obligation to go up to Jerusalem twice a year, in between times they would gather in local meeting places. With the destruction of the First Temple and the exile of the Jews into Babylonia, the synagogue took on a new importance. If one could not have the Temple and its rituals, then other means had to be found to teach and to pray. Even with the rebuilding of the Second Temple, a large number of Jews continued to live outside of Palestine, with large populations in Babylonia, Egypt and throughout the Hellenistic world. The most extensive evidence of synagogues existing throughout the Middle East is to be found in the New Testament, where Paul

Left: Reverend Ezra Stiles' detailed map of Newport (1758). The sketch shows the diversity of religious congregations built around the State House at the center of town. Stiles was a frequent visitor to the Hebrew Synagogue and a good friend of Isaac Touro, Aaron Lopez, and others in the Jewish community.

talks about all the synagogues he preached at in Damascus and on his travels.

The destruction of the Second Temple, and the cessation of all sacrificial ritual, left the synagogue as the main institution around which Jewish life could still organize. The rabbis of this period deliberately adopted many of the customs and rituals of the Temple, such as the reading of the Torah. Prayer became the substitute for the sacrificial rites, and in fact prayer is called avodah, the same name given to the sacrificial system, but now it became the "avodah of the heart."

The synagogue has been known by many names, each reflecting one of its many functions. It has been called a house of prayer, for that is where Jews pray communally. It is a bet midrash, a house of study, for not only are children taught there, but pious adult Jews go there to study Torah and Talmud as well. Another name is bet ha-am, because from its earliest times, the synagogue also served as a communal center, a place for meetings and social activities.

During the Middle Ages there were no great synagogues to match the grandiloquent cathedrals that rose all over Europe. In many places the law forbade Jews from having a synagogue more than one story high, and even the houses of Jews had to be lower than those of their neighbors. The one large synagogue built during this period that defies this tradition is the famous Altneuschul (literally the Old New Synagogue) of Prague built at the end of the 14th century. Only its location, in the very center of a very large Jewish district with no churches nearby, made possible the impressive exterior. It became a model of what other large Jewish communities could do, and with the easing of some restrictions Jews began to build larger and more ornate houses of prayer.

The basic design varied from one building to another, but whether a small one-room shul or a larger building in the Romanesque manner, certain things remained the same. The ark containing the Torah scrolls always stood on the eastern wall, so that the congregation could face toward Jerusalem during services. Women and men did not sit together until the Reform movement of the mid-19th century, so women sat either in a balcony or in a separate section with a screen dividing the sexes (a pattern still followed in Orthodox synagogues). Depending upon the rites followed, the reading table stood immediately in front of the ark (in the Ashkenazic or central European mode, and called a *bimah*) or in the center of the building (in the Sephardic ritual, and called a *tebah*).

Synagogues served more than just the religious, educational and communal needs of the society. They made the statement that a Jewish community lived there. In the English colonies, the pattern was everywhere the same. First a few Jews came, and when their numbers increased they bought land for a burial ground. Then when the community matured, with women and children, they met together as a congregation, holding services either in a house or in rented quarters. Finally, with the accumulation of enough wealth, they built a synagogue. During the colonial era, this pattern could be seen clearly in New York and Newport, and after 1776 in, Philadelphia, Charleston and Richmond.

As late as 1754 (two years after Aaron Lopez arrived), approximately ten to 12 Jewish families lived in Newport, comprising 50 or at the most 60 people. That year they organized a congregation, and took their name—Nefutsé Yisrael, the Scattered of Israel—from a verse in the Book of Isaiah (11:12):

And He will set up an ensign for the nations, and will assemble the dispersed of Israel, and gather together the scattered of Judah from the four corners of the earth.

It appears that they gathered for religious services in the upper story of a house in Duke Street at the corner of Washington Square (then Queen Street), belonging to Moses Lopez and a Dr. Williams. (Years later, after Lopez had sold his share and the house was being repaired, a

copy of a Hebrew book printed in Amsterdam was found under the floorboards, perhaps a sign of how strong the converso tradition remained.) As the city and its Jewish merchants prospered, they yearned for a synagogue, but despite good business conditions, there were in fact only a handful of Jewish families, barely enough to make a minyan. The great wealth of Aaron Lopez was still in the future, and so Newport Jewry relied on help from other Jewish communities in their task. In January 1754, shortly after organizing into a congregation, they appealed to London's Spanish and Portuguese Congregation, known today as the Bevis Marks Synagogue, by then a half-century old and recognized as the mother synagogue of Anglo-Sephardic Jewry. The London congregation prayed for the success of the Newport enterprise, but its treasurer, Mosch de Jacob Franco, informed them that "at the present time it would not be convenient for us, nor are we able to comply with your request." Rather, Franco declared, "May God be the One who assists all, and may he prosper you in your pious plans." The request arrived as England prepared for war with France, and money was tight, but later on the London congregation did make a contribution of £30 sterling.

Within five years, however, Nefutsé Yisrael purchased land for the building. At a meeting the members chose Jacob Rodriguez Rivera, Moses Levy and Isaac Hart to act as trustees for the congregation in acquiring land and securing funds for and overseeing the erection of the synagogue. On June 13, 1759, the trustees formally purchased from Ebenezer Allen, of Sandwich, Massachusetts "One Certain Small parcel or lot of Land Situate Lying and Being in the Township of Newport aforesaid, containing per Estimation Ninety two feet in Front or Breadth and One hundred and six feet in Length or Depth the same Being Butted and Bounded as follows (viz.) Southerly on a Street called Griffin Street, Westerly on Land of Jacob Barney, Northerly on a Street remaining yet to be laid out and Easterly on Land now in the possession and improvement of Matthew Cozzens, be the same more or less within the said Bounds… Together with all fencings, Improvements, ways, waters, Privileges and Appertenances thereto belonging."

The trustees paid £1,500 in local colonial currency, or about $2,410 in current value, a fairly modest sum, but they would need a great deal more to put up the building. They had, in fact, already sent out appeals to other

Sephardic congregations in Jamaica, Curaçao, Suriname, London, and New York. In an eloquent letter to Congregation Shearith Israel in New York (the oldest congregation in the United States), they wrote that they had made arrangements to purchase land, and already had a small sum of money in hand. But they needed more, and hoped their brethren in New York could help:

When we reflect on how much it is our Duty to Instruct children in the Path of Vertuous Religion; and how unhappy the portions must be, of the children and their Parents, who are through necessity educated in a place where they must remain almost Totally uninstructed in our most Holy and Divine Law, our Rites and Ceremonies; and from which place, they may perhaps never have it in their power to depart; when we farther reflect on how much it is our Duty to assist the Distressed; and when we consider the extensive Usefulness of a Charity like this for which we now supplicate assistance; we can entertain no Doubt of your Zeal, to promote this good Work.

In response, on the seventh day of Passover, Shearith Israel had a *nedaba*, or offering in which the congregation raised £149 and 6 pence "towards building at New Port a place of worship to Almighty God," and wished that "you may be a Religious & prosperous Congregation." The Newporters responded "with our most sincere and public thanks," and when Naphtali Hart visited New York the following April, he received the money for transmission to the trustees.

Shearith Israel appears to have been the only congregation to respond so favorably at this time, and the money it raised could not, by itself, finance the new building. Nonetheless, together with local subscription, the community felt confident that it could begin. On August 1, 1759, the Jews of Newport gathered to break ground for their new house of worship. Because of the design of the building, a square sanctuary and an attached school building and sexton's quarters, there were six corners and therefore six cornerstones to be laid. Aaron Lopez received the honor of laying the first one, and his father-in-law, Jacob Rodriguez Rivera the second. Naphtali Hart, Isaac Elizer, Isaac Polock and Naphtali Hart Myers laid the other four, and a special prayer invoking their names is still said every year at services on the eve of Yom Kippur.

Of all the factors that went into the building of the Newport synagogue, none ranks in importance with the selection of the architect, Peter Harrison. In choosing him, the congregation made an inspired choice, and the beauty of his handiwork is still available for all to see and admire.

Born in Yorkshire in 1716 to a Quaker family (he later became an Anglican), Harrison apparently received his architectural training from William and John Etty of York. Unfortunately England entered in a building slump in the 1730s, and for a while he took to the sea as a first mate and later as a captain. Captured by the French and taken to Louisbourg prison in Canada, he spent several months there before being released on a prisoner exchange. While there he secretly copied the plans for the fortress, and on his release gave them to Massachusetts governor William Shirley, who used this information to attack and capture the French bastion in April 1745.

In that same year Harrison and his brother came to Rhode Island, where they received several commissions for drafting plans of harbors and forts. He also met and fell in love with Elizabeth Pelham, the great-granddaughter of Governor Benedict Arnold (grand-father of the later traitor). Since her family thought such a match unsuitable they discouraged his attentions. Despite their efforts, however, Harrison eloped with Elizabeth— already pregnant—and after marriage and the birth of their child returned to Newport, where her family now welcomed him. Through his wife he acquired property known as Harrison's Farm, which is now intersected by Harrison Avenue. He also made contacts that allowed him to utilize the architectural training he had received in England.

The building that made his mark came about by such a contact. The merchant Abraham Redwood, who had come to Newport from Antigua, had been impressed with the ideas of Bishop Berkeley, and in 1746 he and a number of others founded the Redwood Library. Redwood later offered £500 to purchase "useful books suitable for a Public Library… having nothing in view but the Good of Mankind." Another member of the Athenaeum, Henry Collins, donated land for the building, and the group chose Harrison to draw up plans for the building. Harrison took his church-temple design of

Peter Harrison (1716-1775), about 1756. Early American architect and designer of Touro Synagogue, the Redwood Library, and Newport's Brick Market.

the library from the plates of a domed garden pavilion by the Renaissance Italian architect Andrea Palladio, whose four books on architecture served as a bible to several generations of architects.

It would have been natural for the Jews to turn to Harrison when it came time to design and build a sanctuary. Some of the more prosperous merchants belonged to the Redwood, and even those who did not could see the beauty of the building. There were, after all, no professional architects in the colonies at that time. Creative builders added touches of their own in houses, or copied plans from platebooks published in England. Harrison himself seems to have done most of his work without a fee, accepting either the thanks of his clients or a piece of silver plate. He had shown he could design a library and a church (aside from his work in England, he had drawn the plans for the rebuilding of King's Chapel in Boston), but could he design a synagogue?

According to Fiske Kimball, the former director of the Philadelphia Museum of Art, Harrison turned again to his platebooks, and adapted an interior scheme

proposed by Inigo Jones for Whitehall Palace, a two-storied hall with colonnaded aisles, Ionic below, Corinthian above. The plans for the Ark of the Covenant also derived from a platebook. We now know, however, that the Newport synagogue bears striking resemblances to two other contemporary sanctuaries, the Bevis Marks Synagogue of London, built in 1701, and the Great Portuguese Synagogue of Amsterdam, consecrated in 1675. It appears that Harrison took both buildings into account when designing the synagogue for Nefutsé Yisrael.

Architectural historians have pointed out the basic similarities in floor plans between Bevis Marks and Newport, and suggest that Harrison had seen and recalled the London building. The proportions of the two buildings are the same, although Bevis Marks is larger and slightly more elongated, while the three-aisle design as well as other elements are practically identical. If non-Jewish sources are taken into account, it would probably have been the platebooks of Christopher Wren, whose work influenced Bevis Marks' design and with which Harrison would have been very familiar.

Other scholars have suggested that the Amsterdam synagogue may have influenced Harrison, primarily through the number of supporting pillars and placement of objects. Rabbi Morris Gutstein, the long-time rabbi of the synagogue and its primary historian, believes that both the Amsterdam building and Bevis Marks influenced Harrison. "A glance at the contemporary print of the Spanish-Portuguese synagogue at Amsterdam or London," he wrote, "will at once reveal the close similarity between those synagogues and the one in Newport."

Whether Harrison had seen Bevis Marks or not, he knew, as any good architect does, that form must follow function. Since the community of Jews in Newport at the time numbered no more than 60 souls and, even if it should increase as it did in the next decade, its size would probably not be more than double that number in the future. The building had to be sized to the congregation. Of more importance, it had to follow the general layout of a Sephardic house of prayer, in which the *tebah*, or reading table, would have been in the middle, as well as certain rules applicable to all synagogues. The ark had to be on the eastern wall, and because the congregation had to face east while praying, the building had to be set slightly askew from the perpendicular in facing the street. Women had to sit separate from men, and the women's gallery would have been the pattern most familiar to the Jews of Newport. But Harrison did more than just create a shell to house activities; he created an architectural jewel.

Although the plan for the Newport synagogue follows in some ways those of the London and Amsterdam buildings, that may be due more to the fact that all three buildings are Sephardic, and so would have to have certain similarities, such as the placement of the ark containing the Torahs (*hechal*) and the placement of the reader's table (*tebah*) in the middle. (Before the days of electric amplification, some Ashkenazic congregations also had the prayer table in the middle so the reading of the Torah could be heard by everyone.) In Sephardic synagogues the men sit alongside the walls, while in Ashkenazic buildings they utilize rows of seats perpendicular to the side walls. Harrison apparently chose as his working model a two-storied galleried hall, taken from the template in Kent's *Designs of Inigo Jones and Others*. Details for the *hechal*, columns and balustrades came from James Gibb's *Rules for Drawing* and Batty Langley's *Treasury of Designs*. Harrison did not copy these templates slavishly, but like all architects of his time relied heavily on these books for basic designs to adapt to the needs of the client. As one appraisal of his work on the synagogue notes, "In using [these] sources for this building, Peter Harrison proved himself equal not only to achieving fine effects with traditional forms, but capable of creating a new form out of traditional parts."

Harrison enclosed the interior in a severe square hip-roofed brick building decorated only by a sandstone base and belt course, a modillion cornice, and an Ionic columned portico, a unique feature in Newport at that time. The building is unusual in the town for the fact that it does not squarely face the street because, as we noted, the *hechal* had to be placed on an eastern wall facing Jerusalem.

It would be more than four years before the building would be completed. Unlike most of the churches in Newport, the Jews chose to build the synagogue out of brick, and 196,715 bricks had to be imported from England. (In the 19th century, the caretakers of the synagogue painted over the original red brick with a buff-colored paint, adding to the severe appearance of the exterior lines.) Work stopped in 1761, when the congregation apparently ran out of funds, and Naphtali Hart, who had been elected *parnas*, or president, wrote about the dire circumstances to Shearith Israel in New York. After thanking them for their past aid, he noted that the Newporters had been "Greatly disappointed in their Expectations from the Charity of other Congregations and the Cost of the Building too much more than it was Conceived, [so that we] now find [ourselves] unable to Complete the Building." He appealed for aid from New York once again, and apparently Shearith Israel once again came to the rescue, since work resumed on the building.

Shearith Israel, however, had not yet finished helping their brethren in Newport. As the building neared

The Reverend Ezra Stiles (1727-1795), about 1771.
A Congregationalist minister and third president of Yale College, Stiles was a keen observer of colonial life wherever he made his home or traveled. He had a strong interest in the theology and culture of Jewish life in New England.

Touro Synagogue Exterior, 2009.

completion, Congregation Nefutsé Yisrael faced the problem of finding the necessary furniture. After raising all they could locally, the new *parnas*, Moses Lopez wrote in summer 1762 that the building had been completed, except for the porches and the capitals of the pillars. He acknowledged with gratitude the receipt of a *ner tamid*, (a perpetual lamp that hangs near the ark, donated by Samuel Judah), some candlesticks, and 100

pounds of wax from donors in New York, but Newport needed help in securing the necessary furniture for the interior, and once more aid was forthcoming.

Although Lopez had hoped that the consecration of the new building would take place in time for Rosh Hashanah, the Jewish New Year, in 1762, for reasons that are unclear the dedication did not take place until

Touro Synagogue Interior, 2008.

Friday, December 2, 1763, the first day of Chanukah, the Feast of Lights. Men and women filed into the new building, the women going upstairs to their gallery, and a number of non-Jewish notables also had been invited. (It is unclear whether Peter Harrison attended, since in 1761 he had moved to New Haven, where he eventually became collector of customs.) At the appointed time three knocks came from outside upon the closed front door, and the voice of Isaac Touro could be heard chanting in Hebrew "Lift up your heads, O ye gates, and be ye lifted up, ye everlasting doors, that the King of Glory may come in."

From inside the congregation responded, also in Hebrew, "Who is the King of Glory? The Lord of Hosts. He is the King of Glory, Open for me the gates of righteousness, I wish to enter them, I wish to praise the Lord."

At this moment the doors of the building were opened, and Isaac Touro, and the officers of the congregation entered carrying with them the scrolls of the Torah covered in beautiful mantles. Touro then lit the eternal light and chanted the great benediction common to so many Jewish rituals, the *shehecheyanu*—"Blessed art Thou, O Lord our God, King of the Universe, who has given us life, sustained, and brought us to this season."

> *In the Afternoon was the dedication of the Synagogue in this Town…The Order and Decorum, the Harmony & Solemnity of the Musick, together with a handsome Assembly of People, in a Edifice the most perfect of the Temple kind perhaps in America, & splendidly illuminated, could not but raise in the Mind a faint Idea of the Majesty & Grandeur of the Ancient Jewish Worship mentioned in the Scripture. Dr. Isaac de Abraham Touro performed the Service.*
>
> — Ezra Stiles (1763)

Among those present, Dr. Ezra Stiles, then minister of the Second Congregational Church and later president of Yale University, described the new synagogue in terms that, in most particulars, are still accurate today:

The Synagogue is about perhaps 40 foot long and 30 wide, of Brick on a Foundation of Free Stone; it was begun about two years ago, and is now finished except the Porch and the Capitals of the Pillars. The Front Representation of the holy of holies, or its Partition Veil, consists only of wainscoted Breast Work on the East End in the lower part of which four long Doors cover an upright Square Closet the depth of which is about a foot or the thickness of the Wall, and in this Apartment (vulgarly Called the Ark) were deposited three Copies and Rolls of the Pentateuch, written on Vellum or rather tanned Calf Skin; one of these Rolls I was told by Dr. Touro was presented from

Amsterdam and is Two Hundred years old; the Letters have the Rabbinical Flourishes.

A Gallery for the Women runs around the whole inside, except the East End, over which are placed correspondent Columns of the Corinthian order supporting the Ceiling of the Roof. The Depth of the Corinthian Pedestal is the height of the Balustrade which runs around the Gallery. The Pulpit for Reading the Law is a raised Pew with an extended front table; this placed about the center of the Synagogue or nearer the West End, being a Square balustrading Comporting with the Length of the Ark.

On the middle of the North Side and affixed to the Wall is a raised Seat for the Parnas or Ruler, and for the Elders; the Breast and Back interlaid with Chinese Mosaic Work. A Wainscotted Seat runs around Sides of the Synagogue below, and another in the Gallery. There are no other Seats or Pews.

Not everyone shared Stiles' laudatory appraisal of the building. The Rev. Andrew Burnaby had visited the building before its completion, and while agreeing that it would be "extremely elegant within when completed; but the outside is totally spoilt by a school, which the Jews insisted on having annexed to it for the education of their children." The Rev. Burnaby may have known his Palladian principles, but he failed to recognize that even though Newport Jews wanted the very finest in British architecture, they remained, at the same time, cognizant of their Jewishness. They simply had to have a school as part of their commitment to Judaism, and they privileged it above architectural purity or symmetry.

Aside from the capitals, the other major piece of unfinished business consisted of the five brass candelabra that would adorn and light the sanctuary, and that would be hung within a few years following the dedication. (Today, the *ner tamid*, the Eternal Light above the ark, has been converted to electricity; the other candelabra still utilize candles. There are, of course, other sources of light in the building.) It is important to note that the candelabra were donated by Newport's Ashkenazic Jews as well as their Sephardic brethren, clearly indicating the devotion of all to the new building.

The large center candelabrum, given by Jacob Polock, consisted of 12 branches (one for each of the tribes of Israel), with four human figures around the center axis. On either side of the *tebah* (the central reading desk) were two smaller eight-branch candelabra, one the donation of Naphtali Hart Myers and the other from Aaron Lopez, while two six-branched candelabra hung on either side of the *hechal*, both of them given by Abraham, the 12-year-old son of Jacob Rodriguez Rivera.

The *hechal* contains the scrolls of the Torah, the five books of Moses, which are the basis of all Jewish ritual and law. The reading of the Torah is a central feature of the Sabbath morning service, and so a synagogue is not really complete unless it has at least one Torah. Amazingly, the Newport synagogue had three scrolls in the *hechal* at the time of the dedication, and within a few years would gain three more. One of the scrolls, according to tradition, had been the one brought with the original group of Jews who had landed in Newport in 1658. The Spanish and Portuguese Synagogue in Amsterdam had donated a second Torah as its gift to the new congregation, and Aaron Lopez had given a third, one adorned with silver *rimonim*, the decorative crowns and bells atop the wooden poles holding the scrolls. Within a short period of time, Newport received another Torah from the Bevis Marks synagogue in London, and the trustees of the religious school as well as an individual identified as Ebar bar Shelomoh (Ebar the son of Solomon) both contributed Torahs. In addition to these six owned outright by the congregation, there were others loaned to it. Shearith Israel in New York lent one that had originally been lent to the congregation in Savannah, Georgia, while another belonged to Jacob Rodriguez Rivera that he bequeathed to his son Abraham.

At least two sets of *rimonim*, atop the Torah had been made by the famed New York silversmith Myer Myers, and possibly a third was his handiwork as well, and two sets had been donated by the Hays and Myers family. Other members of the local community and members of Jewish congregations in both the new world and Europe donated various items such as a charity box, a clock, and later on, two oil paintings. One, of the tablets of the Ten Commandments, hangs on the wall

directly above the ark containing the Torahs, another painting, of Moses, Aaron and the Ten Commandments, with a Spanish translation of the Hebrew under each commandment, hangs in another part of the building. In due time the capitals of the pillars were finished, a stove installed, and the other necessities of the sanctuary and the attached school building secured. When everything had been completed, the cost exceeded £2000 sterling, a considerable amount of money for the time, and greater than had been anticipated when Nefutsé Yisrael had embarked on the venture.

In fact, the Jewish community of Newport did not have this money at the time. A decade later men like Aaron Lopez would invest ten times that amount in a sailing

Torah Scrolls on deer or calf skin, about 1550.

venture, but in 1762 they had to secure a mortgage at eight percent interest to pay for a good part of their new edifice. To make matters worse, the onset of the French and Indian War in early 1763 triggered a depression, and Newport Jewry once again had to go asking other congregations for help. A few days after Rosh Hashanah 1764, the Jews of Newport sent the following appeal to Congregation Mikveh Israel of Curaçao:

> For two years we have just about managed to collect enough to pay the interest at eight percent, an expenditure which, when added to the annual expenses involved in the maintenance of the synagogue, has proved extremely difficult for this small congregation in such adverse times. The third annual due date of the mortgage having arrived, and …[in view of the fact] that it will be impossible for us not only to pay the principal, but even the interest, we find it necessary to appeal to our brethren, and to inform them of our deplorable situation, especially when we consider the great risk of eventually losing our valued building…
>
> We flatter ourselves that since the practice of mitzvoth [good deeds of religious merit] is so deeply engrained in your spirit, you will unanimously agree to come to the aid of this effort. May God lead you to such action and may He be pleased to recompense your large congregation with long life, increased favor, and prosperity for many years.

It appears that these appeals, like those before them, elicited help, since the congregation managed to meet its obligations and pay off the mortgage.

With the dedication of the building the congregation also changed its name. No longer Nefutsé Yisrael, the "Scattered of Israel," they would now be known as Yeshuat Israel, the "Salvation of Israel." The building itself remains an architectural gem, a worthy legacy of that small Jewish community in pre-revolutionary Newport.

Unfortunately, relatively little is known of the man who led the dedication services, Isaac de Abraham Touro. Although Ezra Stiles speaks of him quite often in his diary, those are details of conversations rather than biographical information about the man who served as spiritual leader of Newport Jewry in the 15 or so years before the Revolution. Born in 1738, most probably on one of the Caribbean islands to a family that had escaped the Inquisition, he went to Amsterdam to study at one of the schools maintained by the large Jewish community there. It is unclear whether he came to Newport by chance around 1759, or whether the Jews of

Newport, as they prepared to build a synagogue, wrote to Amsterdam asking for someone to come and serve as their *hacham* (the Sephardic term for rabbi). Prior to his arrival it appears that services had been led either by a member of the congregation, or on rare occasions by an itinerant rabbi. Touro arrived after the basic plans for the building had been agreed upon, but it is likely that he influenced the interior design, perhaps informing Peter Harrison of some of the characteristics of the large Amsterdam synagogue. It is quite clear that he presided over the impressive dedication service.

Whether Touro had actually gone through a formal course of rabbinical training is doubtful, and it would not have been unusual for a person with good training in Torah to serve as teacher for a small frontier congregation. Technically, he may have been little more than the officiating *hazzan* or cantor, subject to the authority of the lay leadership, but to Newport's non-Jews Touro represented the Jewish equivalent of their own ministers, and they treated him with great respect. It appears that he got along well both with the members of the congregation and non-Jewish townsfolk as well. A singer with a fine voice, he joined a number of local organizations, including the Masons, and had a good reputation for hospitality to strangers and to those in need.

One of the main purposes of the community in building the synagogue had been to provide a place of learning for their children, and this task Touro took over quite successfully. Ezra Stiles noted in his diary that he attended evening services on January 12, 1770, when a young boy read the entire evening service as part of his bar mitzvah, his initiation into the community. "This is the first Instance of [bar mitzvah at] the Synagogue at Newport." At other times Stiles noted that children, even those under thirteen, read from the Bible in Hebrew, as "Mr. Rivera's little son 8 or 9 aet. Read the first Chapter of Ezekial."

Right: The Reverend Isaac Touro (1738–1783), about 1767. First Hazzan of Congregation Yeshuat Israel.

Stiles, the minister of the Second Congregational Church in Newport from 1755 to 1776, had an omnivorous intellectual appetite, and after receiving a Doctor of Divinity degree from Edinburgh in 1765, he decided to learn Hebrew. Apparently he progressed slowly until Touro came to town. The two men soon became not only teacher and student, but fast friends. Stiles started attending the services, perhaps, as some suggest, to scoff and seek means of converting the Jews, but stayed on to be intrigued by Judaism and its rituals and become a student of them. Touro and Stiles visited each other's homes, walked together in the streets discussing topics of mutual interest such as theology, prophecy and biblical interpretation, and studied Hebrew and the Bible together. Later on when Stiles, as president of Yale, taught Hebrew to his students, they found the language "very disagreeable" and objected to memorizing Psalms in Hebrew. He told them that these "would be the first we should hear sung in heaven, and that he would be ashamed that any of his pupils should be entirely ignorant of that holy language."

Stiles refers to Touro by a number of titles, including "*Chuzzan* from Amsterdam," "Jew Priest," "*Chazan*," "*Huzan*," or occasionally "Mr.." Once only does he call him "Dr." and never refers to him as "Rabbi" or even "*Hacham*." On the memorial tablet erected by his son Abraham, he is referred to as "Rev'd Isaac Touro, the able and faithful Minister of the Congregation Yeshuat Israel."

Since the synagogue had no home for him, Touro rented a six-room house from George Buckmaster on High Street (now Division Street). To that house in 1773 he brought his bride, Reyna Hays, the daughter of the prominent New York merchant Judah Hays and a sister of Moses Michael Hays. Both Hays men had extensive business connections in Newport. Reyna bore her husband four children, two sons, Abraham and Judah, whose generosity would later play an important role in the history of the Newport synagogue, a boy Nathan who died in infancy, and a daughter, Rebecca, who later in life would marry Joshua Lopez, one of Aaron's sons. Just before she died in December 1833, Rebecca made known her wish to be buried in Newport. Her funeral in the synagogue, as the local paper noted, was "the first

time for the last 40 years that the ceremony of the Jews has been performed in the Synagogue."

A Tory in sympathy, Isaac Touro did not leave Newport at the outbreak of the Revolution, but continued to minister to Yeshuat Israel until 1780, when the community had become so decimated and impoverished that it could not longer support a *hacham*. He went to New York, where he briefly served as interim *hazzan* of Shearith Israel. For unknown reasons, he soon left New York and went to Jamaica, perhaps his birthplace, and died there in 1784. Although his remains were never brought back to Newport, when his wife (who had gone to Boston to live with her brother after his death) died, their son Abraham put up a monument over her grave in Newport dedicated to both of his parents.

The man who married Isaac Touro and Reyna Hays on June 30, 1773, played a small but noteworthy role in the pre-Revolutionary life of Newport Jewry. On March 8, 1773, the Reverend Ezra Stiles attended Purim services and recorded in his diary his first impression of Haijm Isaac Karigal (Carigal):

> *There I saw Rabbi Carigal I judge aet. 45, lately from the city of Hebron, the Cave of the Macpelah in the Holy Land. He was one of the two persons that stood by the Chusan at the Taubauh or Reading Desk while the Book of Esther was read. He was dressed in a red garment with the usual Phylacteries and habiliments, the white silk Surplice; he wore a high brown furr Cap, had a long Beard. He has the appearance of an ingenious & sensible Man.*

Haijm Karigal had been born in Hebron in 1733, but from the early 1750s on had traveled widely in the Middle East, Europe and the New World, where he occasionally served as an itinerant preacher. He only stayed in Newport for about four months, enough time to establish a close friendship with Ezra Stiles, officiate at Isaac Touro's wedding, and preach several sermons, only one of which has been preserved. Karigal and Stiles spent an extraordinary amount of time together, with the former providing the Congregational minister with many details about the Holy Land and its Jewish population at the time (about 1,000 families and 12 synagogues), and the two discussing the finer points of theology. On one day Stiles noted that he "discoursed

Haijm Isaac Karigal

Haijm Karigal had been born in Hebron in 1733, but from the early 1750s on had traveled widely in the Middle East, Europe and the New World, where he occasionally served as an itinerant preacher. He only stayed in Newport for about four months, enough time to establish a close friendship with Ezra Stiles, officiate at Isaac Touro's wedding, and preach several sermons, only one of which has been preserved.

Rabbi Raphael Haijm Isaac Karigal, 1772.

May 28, 1773

Carigal preached a sermon at the Shavuot service in Spanish (or perhaps in Ladino) that lasted three-quarters of an hour on "the salvation of Israel," before an audience that included not only the members of the congregation, several local officials including Governor Joseph Wanton, Judges Oliver and Auchmuty, as well as the Reverend Stiles. The sermon impressed the audience, more for the delivery and drama than for the content, which few in the audience understood.

on Ventriloquism & the Witch of Endor and the Reality of bringing up Samuel. [Karigal] had not heard of Ventriloquism before and still doubted it."

On May 28, 1773, Karigal preached a sermon at the Shavuot service in Spanish (or perhaps in Ladino) that lasted three-quarters of an hour on "the salvation of Israel," before an audience that included not only the members of the congregation, several local officials including Governor Joseph Wanton, Judges Oliver and Auchmuty, as well as the Reverend Stiles. The sermon impressed the audience, more for the delivery and drama than for the content, which few in the audience understood. Karigal used no notes, but spoke

extemporaneously. As he later told Stiles, he worked it out in his head, and "sealed" it there. At the urging of Stiles and others, Karigal wrote it out in Spanish, and despite his urging that it not be published, after he left Newport the Jewish community had it translated into English and published.

On leaving Newport, Karigal went to Barbados and took up a rabbinical post there. Apparently he continued to correspond with Stiles until his death in 1777. After Stiles became president of Yale, he suggested to Aaron Lopez in 1781 that "the affectionate respect I bear to the memory of…the Rabbi Carigal has made me to wish that his picture might be deposited in the library of this college." Although Lopez had by then fled Newport, he immediately agreed to Stiles' request, and Stiles arranged for Samuel King to paint a portrait of Karigal that for many years hung in the Yale library. The portrait was completed after Lopez's death, and Jacob Rodriguez Rivera, Lopez's father-in-law, who had paid for part of the portrait, now offered to pay for an appropriate frame as well.

The decade or so before the American Revolution constituted not only the golden age of Newport commerce, but the best of times for its small Jewish community. Although still deprived of political rights, they seemed to face no impervious social or economic barriers. One must at all times keep in mind that despite the great wealth and influence of men like Aaron Lopez and Jacob Rivera, the community itself apparently never consisted of more than 25 to 30 families, and a total population of men, women and children of between 125 and 150 souls. Made up of both Sephardim and Ashkenazim, all agreed to the Sephardic ritual that had determined the internal architecture of the synagogue. During the construction period, the Sephardic Jacob Rodriguez Rivera served as *parnas* of the congregation for part of the time, and was succeeded in that office by the Ashkenazic Naphtali Hart. The community enjoyed the services of a popular *hazzan* during these years, and their children received a solid Jewish education.

The community apparently had the service of a local *shochet*, or butcher who slaughtered animals according to Jewish ritual requirements. Aaron Lopez's many ventures included the export of kosher beef to Jamaica, while some of his colleagues in Newport sent meat to Suriname and Barbados. As late as 1787 it appears that Jewish merchants in Newport were still shipping certified kosher beef to Suriname. The small size of the community, however, meant that it could not support a *mohel*, the person who performs ritual circumcision (*brit milah*) on newborn male children. For this they had to rely on Abraham Israel Abrahams of New York, who served the members of Shearith Israel, but engaged in what can only be described as circuit riding that took him as far north as Newport. In July 1755, when Sarah Lopez delivered a son Joseph, her husband Aaron wrote to New York to have Abrahams come to Newport to

do the *brit*. A variety of factors kept Abrahams from making the trip, so that young Joseph would not be circumcised until the following February. On the same trip, Abrahams performed the *brit* on Joseph's cousin Aaron, the son of Moses Lopez. When Aaron's brother Miguel and his three sons escaped from the Inquisition and came to Newport, Aaron sent for the New Yorker to come to Newport again and circumcise all four males. The sons ranged in age from 17 to 28, and the father was then 56.

Keeping the Sabbath in predominantly Christian communities often was a great burden on colonial Jews, but keep the Sabbath most of them did. As we noted, Aaron Lopez closed his shops on Friday afternoon in time to get home and prepare for the Sabbath, and he kept them closed not only all day Saturday, but on Sunday as well out of respect for the Christian Sabbath. None of his ships reportedly left port on the Sabbath. He also closed his business for all of the major Jewish holidays, and when an out-of-town client came to Newport one April, he later wrote that he had stopped by the store but "it happened to be on holy days and could not see you." When his brother Moses traveled to Charleston on business, he dropped a short note to Aaron that he was unable to "write more fully because now it is almost Sabbath."

From all reports, it appeared that Jews and Christians lived harmoniously side-by-side. There was no ghetto in Newport, and Jewish merchants lived in houses befitting their wealth and rank next to Christians of similar standing. Despite the official position of the colony as a Christian commonwealth, there appears to have been little overt anti-Semitism. Jews intermingled with Christians in the Masonic lodges, the Redwood, and other social organizations, and they did business together. The ending of the French and Indian Wars in 1763 ushered in a period of great prosperity in which all of the merchants of Newport participated.

Unfortunately, the golden age would soon come to an end as the American colonies, reluctantly at first and then with greater commitment, sought to win independence from Great Britain.

CHAPTER 5

The American Revolution and Its Aftermath

Comte de Rochambeau and General George Washington.
In 1780, Commander-in-Chief Washington offered Newport, RI
to the French as their military headquarters in the United States.
Count Rochambeau (Jean-Baptiste Donatien de Vimeur) the French
commander and Washington met there in 1781 to plan the attack on
the British in Yorktown, Virginia.

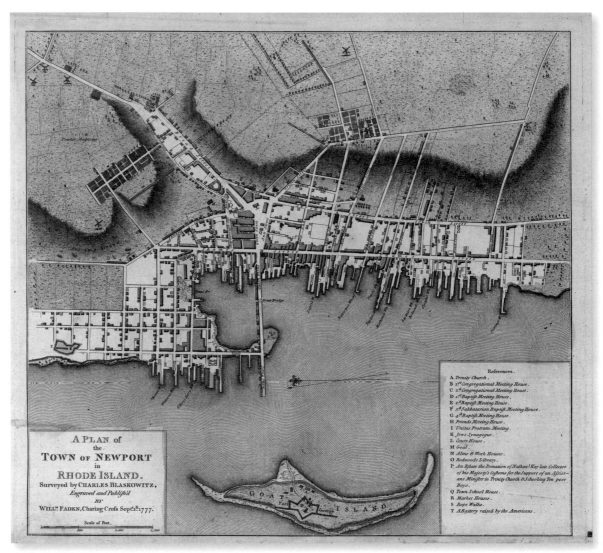

A plan of the town of Newport in Rhode Island, 1777. Newport was under British and Hessian control from October 1776 to November 1779. Over 300 wood structures were destroyed, Long Wharf was devastated, and churches were gutted or used as hospitals. Six months after the enemy evacuated the town, General Washington turned Newport into the headquarters for his new French allies under General Jean-Baptiste Donatien de Vimeur Comte de Rochambeau. The French fleet arrived on 11 July 1780 with their General and 5,000 troops. Rochambeau and Washington met in Newport in 1781 and planned their attack on British General Cornwallis. The French troops marched out of town on 9 June 1781 headed directly to Yorktown.

{ CHAPTER 5 }

The American Revolution and Its Aftermath

THE AMERICAN REVOLUTION ENDED THE GOLDEN AGE OF Newport, including that of its Jewish community. Although quite a few Jews held Tory sympathies, a majority backed the struggle for independence. After the British occupied the city in 1776, many of them fled, never to return. The end of the war found the Newport economy in ruins, its leading merchants bankrupt, and its future bleak.

Although some Jews would continue to live in Newport into the early 19th century, the community itself soon faded away. Ironically, the most prized moment in the history of Newport Jewry—perhaps in the history of American Jewry—came during this period of decline: George Washington's famed Letter to the Hebrew Congregation in Newport.

The end of the French and Indian War in 1763 left Great Britain the dominant power in North America, with French possessions in the New World reduced to a few islands in the Caribbean. But the costs of the war also left England with enormous debt, one beyond the ability of the already heavily taxed population of the Mother Country to pay. The colonies had paid little or nothing to support the war, and the government in London had reimbursed the colonial assemblies for any expenses incurred on behalf of the army.

When George Grenville became George III's chief minister in 1763, he not only had to grapple with the debt but with annual costs of £300,000 for the administration and defense of the American colonies. The colonies had prospered over the past century thanks in large measure to the mercantile system that protected their trade within the British imperial system. Even the war had not done much to harm that prosperity, since many colonists—especially in New England—had been quite willing to continue their trade with the French West Indies during the conflict. To Grenville the solution to at least part of his problem was simple and clear—the colonies had to pay their own way. The amounts that would have been raised in the Stamp Act of 1765 and other revenue measures proposed over the next decade would not, in fact, have covered all the colonial costs, but would have eased His Majesty's Government's financial problems. Moreover, the amount would have been only a slight burden on the colonists. Nonetheless many of the colonists resisted all efforts by London to tax them, continued and indeed increased their smuggling to avoid the duties imposed by the Navigation Acts, and slowly came to the conclusion that, as Richard Henry Lee of Virginia put it, "these United Colonies are, and of right ought to be, free and independent states."

Rhode Islanders had indeed prospered under the imperial system, but they, like their fellow New England merchants, had ignored the Navigation Acts as much as possible. They smuggled goods into the many coves along Narragansett Bay by night to evade British customs sloops, some of which deliberately looked the other way thanks to persistent bribery on the part of the colonists. Even though they disliked and evaded the new taxes proposed by Grenville, iconoclastic Rhode Island refused to join with her sister colonies in the many protests and boycotts that occurred between 1765 and the issuance of the Declaration of Independence in July 1776.

When a Mr. Robinson came to Newport in 1764 to take up his post as Collector of Customs, Ezra Stiles noted that his official salary was £100 sterling. Yet merchants told Stiles that Robinson made at least another 6,000 dollars a year through bribes, and that his underlings in the Customs Office each made at least 3,000 dollars. "We all pay them," said one merchant, "and are glad to get off in that manner." If no bribe were paid and one of His Majesty's cutters did intercept a colonial smuggler, the undermanned British would often be fought off by its crew.

The Jewish merchants of Newport were no better and no worse than their Christian counterparts, and indeed, as has been noted, were often partners in various shipping ventures, both licit and illicit. One captain in Aaron Lopez's employ informed him of a close call in Nevis, where British cutters had seized two vessels with more goods on board than listed in their cargo manifests, and he had narrowly avoided being boarded as well.

The difference between Newport and Providence merchants and those in the other colonies is that the Rhode Islanders had little interest in paying any more heed to the various colonial boycotts of British goods than they did to the Navigation Acts. Whatever their religious beliefs, they all subscribed to a policy of free trade and making money, and neither British financial needs nor colonial resistance ought to get in their way. The colonies, including Rhode Island, established their first non-importation agreement after the Stamp Act of 1765, a device that worked primarily because of pressure on the Grenville government from British merchants who suffered serious damage to their trade with the colonists.

To make up for the lost revenue, Parliament passed the Townshend Acts in 1767, triggering another round of protests and boycotts of English goods that in 1770 led to their repeal, with the exception of the tax on tea. Rhode Island and New Hampshire, however, refused to join in this non-importation agreement, and their merchants continued to trade with the British until the other colonies placed an embargo on goods coming in and out of Newport. As a result Rhode Island merchants reluctantly agreed to join the non-importation agreement.

While we do not have letters or other documents telling us very much about what Jewish merchants thought

during this time, we do have the extensive records of Aaron Lopez, and his views, as the leading merchant of the community, may well have expressed those of his fellow congregants. When he had to, Lopez went along with the non-importation agreements, but it is clear that he felt uncomfortable in the events leading up to the break with the Mother Country. Lopez had fled from the Portuguese Inquisition, and in British-ruled America had been able not only to practice his religion freely but to prosper as well. While it is true that Rhode Island authorities had refused Lopez's petition for naturalization, he had little trouble getting it in Massachusetts. Lopez did not see in George III the royal brute that Thomas Paine described. To the contrary, he seemed to fear the actions of the would-be rebels far more than that of the English crown, and complained to business associates that "our sanguine Sons of Liberty [had] debarr'd us from an importation of English goods." As the colonies and England moved toward what appeared to be an inevitable conflict, Aaron Lopez "fervently invoke[d God's] mercies and pray[ed] for our preservation from the impending calamities that at present seem to threaten this infatuated meridian."

Regarding the hated tea tax, which eventually led to the Boston Tea Party, the colonies agreed not to purchase any more tea from the East India Company. Rhode Island, while outwardly compliant, apparently still dealt in the commodity. Although nearly all merchants violated the boycott, some people blamed the Jews for breaking the non-importation agreement in Rhode Island. In Boston, the hotbed of rebellion, irate merchants claimed that the culprits in Newport were "chiefly Jews," and Ezra Stiles noted that "five or six Jews & three or 4 Tories" had drawn "down Vengeance upon" a whole country. Stiles singled out his friend Aaron Lopez as the chief culprit, and it was undisputed that he enjoyed a rather privileged place with customs officials. None of his captains had to swear at the Customs House that their cargoes did not contain contraband, while British officials strictly exacted oaths from all those who had agreed not to import British goods.

An article in the *Newport Mercury* noted that "Mr. Aaron Lopez, owner of the Ship Jacob . . . has assured us, in Riting [sic], that said ship has no India Tea on board and that he thinks himself happy in giving such assurance." At the same time, one of his competitors, Peleg Clarke, was busily smuggling tea into the colony, and apparently so was Lopez. An invoice dated March 4, 1774 listed ten chests of Bohea tea shipped to "St. Eustasia on account of Aaron Lopez."

The tendency to blame Jews for breaking the non-importation agreement can, and has, been interpreted as a sign that even after all their years living in Newport, and despite the high esteem they apparently enjoyed among Christian merchants, in times of crisis old anti-Semitic sentiments would still surface. John Collins, a member of the local non-importation committee, despite Lopez's assurances, a month later still declared his distrust of the Newport Jews, and declared, "Our Danger is from among ourselves, from the Circumcised and Uncircumcised Jews, that they may import tea." James Otis of Boston, describing a group of reformers who wanted to end illicit Rhode Island trade by establishing a Royalist government referred to the "little, dirty, drinking, contaminated knot of thieves . . . made up of Turks, Jews, and other infidels," even though he knew there were no Jews—or Turks for that matter—in the group. Jews were not the only Newport merchants to ignore the non-importation agreement, but in a small city, they remained visible, and still outsiders, despite their apparent integration into the community. The fact that Jews prior to the Revolution were totally barred from holding office and even from voting may have contributed to their sense of pursuing self-interest over the so-called "public good."

By 1774 a rupture with England seemed inevitable. The Boston Tea Party had been the last straw for His Majesty's Government, which retaliated with a series of measures, known as the Intolerable Acts, designed to bring the rebellious colonies to heel. The measures failed in that purpose, and in July 1776 the colonies declared their independence. For Lopez, Rivera, Hart and others, a choice had to be made—whether to remain as loyal subjects to George III or to cast their lot with the rebellion.

Outside of Boston, which had been put under strict control in late 1774, life in the colonies remained more or less normal in the months leading up to the war. In Newport merchants did what they had always done—sent their ships out to sea to make money. In January 1775, Lopez formed a partnership with the Quaker merchant Francis Rotch and Richard Smith of Boston. The three men outfitted almost 20 ships at a cost of £40,000 to go whaling in the Falkland Islands off the coast of southern South America. By the time the fleet sailed in early September, the battles of Lexington and Concord had been fought, and the British fleet had Boston under siege. Lopez and his partners laid their plans carefully, and knew that the fleet would often be operating in waters patrolled by British warships. After whaling and sealing, the fleet would make its way back to the Dutch island of St. Eustatius (with its sizable Jewish community), where it would pick up contraband to smuggle back through the British blockade. As one scholar so accurately described it, "It was gamble piled upon gamble, a desperate venture at best." And it turned into a disaster, with most of the boats lost to the sea, and the rest captured by the British.

At some point, perhaps in late 1775 or early 1776, Aaron Lopez decided to throw in his lot with the patriot cause. He did so reluctantly, but after 20 years of living in Rhode Island, he found that his loyalties lay more with his home than with the monarch in far off London. We have a letter written to him in 1777 by his agent and friend Benjamin Wright, in response to one (now lost) that Lopez had sent to him. Clearly Wright reflected Lopez's views when he wrote: "I sincerely condole with you on the melancholly [sic] situation of that once happy country [America], & readily admit there is no real happiness to be expected in this frail world."

> *Poor Newport, what is to be its fate at last; I fear destruction. Its inhabitants are already scattered to the four corners of the earth. My good sir, when I reflect on the happy days we have spent there, and with what ease and pleasure yourself and some others went through a multiplicity of business, I can hardly persuade myself that I am awake.*
>
> — Joseph Anthony to Aaron Lopez (1779)

British warships anchored in Newport's harbor in early 1776, and according to one report, "have put almost a total end to commerce; have committed repeated depredations in different parts of the colony; have kept our coast constantly alarmed, and obliged the residents to keep almost continually under arms." The precipitous drop in commerce hurt not only the pockets of merchants and artisans, but the coffers of the colonial government as well. Many residents fled Newport—the town's population dropped from 11,000 in 1775 to less than half that number a year later—and left the assembly with the problem of taking care of those who could not flee and were, for the most part, poor.

Former governor Samuel Ward, now a delegate to the Continental Congress, urged residents on the island to take themselves and as much property as they could carry to places of greater safety, a sentiment formally endorsed by the General Assembly.

Aaron Lopez took that advice, and quit Newport. He moved his business and family first to Portsmouth, Rhode Island in early 1776. A year later, after the British had occupied Newport, he moved again, to Providence, and from there went to Leicester, Massachusetts in the summer of 1777, where he had earlier established some business interests. There they were joined by his father-in-law Jacob Rodriguez Rivera, Abraham Mendes and nearly 30 members of their families and numerous servants. Until his death in 1782, Lopez did business out of Leicester and traveled in the states, trying to straighten out his accounts, collect monies owed to him, and regain possession of his ships seized by American privateers.

Sir Henry Clinton and his British soldiers occupied Newport without resistance on December 8, 1776, and stayed there for three years. While certainly not an inhumane occupation—there were no executions—there was a great deal of damage done, especially when the British repelled an effort to capture the city by a combined French and American force. The Jewish community in town was split in their loyalties. In particular the Hart, Polack, and Myers families chose to evacuate to British or Dutch controlled territories, and maintained a low profile presence in town during the occupation. Even Isaac Touro, argued to the patriots

that he could not be a Tory since he had never naturalized as a British citizen (he owed his allegience to "the States of Holland"). However, he took his family and left Newport in 1779 when the British evacuated. They moved to the safe-haven of New York, then still under royalist control. In 1781 Touro petitioned both the King's governor-general and the Congregation in London for the funds to move his family to Jamaica.

After the British left, the new Rhode Island state assembly in 1780 confiscated Isaac Hart's and other loyalist property, and they fled to British-controlled land on Long Island. Of Myer Polack, Edmund Burke spoke eloquently of him before the House of Commons:

> He had formerly lived on Rhode Island; and, because he had imported tea contrary to the command of the Americans, he was stripped of all he was worth, and driven out of the island; his brother shared in his misfortunes, but did not survive them; his death increased the cares of the survivor, as he got an additional family, and his brother's children, to provide for. Another Jew married his sister; and both of them following the British Army, had for their loyalty some lands given to them ... on Long Island, by Sir William Howe. They built a kind of fort there, to defend themselves, but it was soon after attacked and carried by the Americans, and not a man who defended it escaped either death or captivity.

According to the official English report, Hart was "murdered at Long Island [December 1780] with the greatest brutality by the rebels for his attachment to Great Britain." His brother, Jacob Hart managed to reach England with his family, where their loyalty was rewarded with an annual pension of £40, but Jacob and his wife both died within a short period of time. Polock survived and moved to St. Eustatius, but never recouped his wealth.

Right: Moses Michael Hays (1739-1805). Hays was a patriot, merchant, banker, Grand Master Freemason, and founder of several cultural institutions. His sister became the wife of Hazzan Isaac de Abraham Touro and his close brother-in-law was American silversmith, Myer Myers.

Isaac Touro found himself without a congregation after the war began, since most of the Newport Jews who supported the patriot cause had left town. Before the British abandoned Newport, he moved to New York, where in the absence of the regular *hazzan*, he served Shearith Israel in that capacity for about two years. He did not remain in New York, but, perhaps hoping that a warmer climate would benefit his health, returned to Jamaica, where he died on January 8, 1784. His death, however, did not cut the cord binding the Touro family to Newport, and both his sons, Abraham and Judah, would be munificent benefactors of the synagogue in the following century.

The Tories amongst Newport Jewry appear to have been far outnumbered by those who subscribed to the patriot cause. Moses Isaacs, who in 1781 would entertain General George Washington in his home, joined the army, as did a relative, Abraham Isaacs, as well as Abraham Seixas, and Samuel Benjamin. Aaron Lopez received the sum of £22 for gunpowder and a whaleboat he gave to the colony, and Jacob Isaacs provided several small cannon (probably taken off smuggling vessels). Many of those who fled the city did so for the simple reason that they supported the patriot cause, and feared retribution should the British occupy Newport.

The war ruined not only the Jewish community of Newport, but the town itself. One merchant, William Ellery, claimed that when the British left Newport 500 buildings had been burned, and considerable property taken by the soldiers. "All the destructible property I had there," he cried, "was utterly destroyed." A British visitor to the town in 1785, Joseph Hadfield, noted that as a result of the "devastation of war . . . the poverty of the inhabitants will be an insuperable barrier for at least some time." The Long Wharf, the pride of Newport in its golden era, had been completely destroyed, as had most of the warehouses and stores along the waterfront. Where in the early 1770s hundreds of ships had sailed from Newport, Hadfield saw only 20 vessels in the overseas trade and some 30 in the coastal trade, a total smaller than the individual fleets of the great merchants such as Aaron Lopez and others had owned before the war. Nor was it likely that even if the destruction had not been so great, Newport would have been able to recapture its pre-war commercial position. The economic

recession that struck the United States in the early 1780s bore down particularly hard on the type of commerce that had once engaged Newport shipping. Without, as Hadfield noted, "persons of consequence in the mercantile line here," Newport became a shadow of its former greatness, and business leadership in Rhode Island shifted to Providence. The three wealthiest men in pre-war Newport—Aaron Lopez, George Rome, and Joseph Wanton—never returned to the city, while the Brown and Russell families never left Providence. About the only good thing for Newport Jewry that can be said to have resulted from the war was the partial end of their political segregation.

Moses Michael Hays had resided in Newport since 1769. A prosperous merchant, he was also a Freemason who was instrumental in bringing Scottish Rite Masonic lodges to the East Coast and Caribbean. On July 11, 1776, one week after the Continental Congress declared independence, several officers of the Rhode Island Brigade of the Continental Army accused Hays and many other Newport men of possibly being "inimical" to the patriot cause. The Rhode Island legislature had passed a bill allowing members of the State Assembly and active officers of the military to accuse another person of disloyalty. The accuser did not have to offer proof in support of his charge, but once the accusation had been made, the suspect had to appear before a committee of the General Assembly and swear an oath of allegiance to the Revolutionary cause.

This presented a problem in religiously diverse Rhode Island. Not every citizen could in good conscience swear an oath. The Quakers, for example, do not swear oaths on the grounds that taking one implies they might otherwise lie, when their religious scruples demand that they always tell the truth. Some Jews also refuse to swear civil oaths, claiming that oaths are reserved for promises made to God, not to one's fellow humans. The assembly recognized this problem, and therefore agreed to accept other forms of affirmation of loyalty.

Hays could easily have met this requirement, and only a month before had endorsed the justness of the patriot cause in writing. Aside from the insult of being named as "inimical" by an unnamed source, Hays had another reason why he refused to take the oath, even though he recognized the dangers of this action. If he failed to take the oath, he could have lost the right to bear arms, possibly his freedom, and he and his family might well have been expelled from the newly declared State of Rhode Island. Nonetheless, when he appeared before the General Assembly on July 12, 1776, he declared:

> I have and ever shall hold the strongest principles and attachments to the just rights and privileges of this my native land. . . . I decline subscribing to the Test [oath] at present for these principles: First, that I… call for my accusers and proof of conviction. Second, that I am an Israelite and am not allowed the liberty of a vote, or a voice in common with the rest of the voters… Thirdly, because the Test is not general… and Fourthly…the General Assembly of this [colony has] never in this contest taken any notice or countenance respecting the Society of Israelites to which I belong.

The defiant Hays invoked two principles that had long been embedded in Rhode Island's civic culture: non-discrimination against members of religious minorities, and acceptance of them as full members of the body politic. Judaism had been tolerated in Rhode Island almost from the colony's beginnings, and Jews had never suffered the type of social and economic fetters so common in the Old World. At the same time, they had not been allowed to become full citizens. Hays was in effect telling the Assembly: if you want me to take this oath, then you must also accept me as a citizen with full rights.

Hays did not hear from the Assembly for several days, but when they met again in General session on July 17 he delivered a second petition:

> I ask of your Honors the Rights and Privileges due other free citizens…and again implore that the justice of your Honors may interfere in my behalf and will give me leave again to call for the cause and my accusation of Inimicality, that I may have an opportunity of vindication.

Hays finally did sign the loyalty oath. The previous day, the Assembly had passed a "more general" act requiring a loyalty oath from all male persons in the state over 21

years old, not just those suspected by their neighbors. While signing this revised oath may have certified Hays as a patriot, it still did not grant him the vote. Just before the British occupied Newport that December, Hays moved his household to a temporary residence in South Kingston, RI, returning to Newport early in 1780 just after the British evacuation. In 1782, he moved the family and his business to Boston.

The Assembly, however, responded to the force of Moses Michael Hays' arguments—which some scholars believe to be the first case on religious equality before the law and minority rights in the newly formed United States of America. The following year the Assembly enfranchised the Jews, declaring that they were no longer to be "deprived… of the invaluable rights of free citizens," as they had "hitherto been." Interestingly the Assembly did not grant Catholics the same rights and privileges as Protestants until 1783. Although Jews could now vote, they still could not hold office, and it was not until 1842 and the final overthrow of the old charter by Dorr's Rebellion that Jews finally achieved full political equality in the state.

The census of 1782 indicated the presence of only six Jewish families in Newport. The Lopez, Rivera, and Mendes families were still in Leicester, but getting ready to move back. Some other Jewish families also filtered back, but ten years after the British occupation ended, estimates vary from somewhere between ten and 20 Jewish families, and from 75 to perhaps 100 individuals. During the 1780s Jewish as well as Christian merchants tried to replenish their businesses and fortunes, sending some ships to the West Indies and attempting to start up ship-building companies. Joseph Lopez and Jacob Rodriguez Rivera restored some of their Atlantic and West Indies trade, and Moses Seixas also began trading in the Caribbean. But just as the entrepreneurial spirit of pre-war Newport had fostered individual success and had, in turn, been replenished by it, so now the dim prospects of the town put a damper on these efforts.

One can only speculate what might have been if Aaron Lopez had returned to Newport. He had managed to move a fair amount of his wealth with him to Leicester, bought land there, and had built a large and elegant building that housed both his family's living quarters and his store. Over time he purchased additional land, perhaps 80 to 100 acres in and around the town. The local townspeople would remember the large Lopez, Rivera and Mendes families as quiet and good neighbors, who rigidly kept the practices required by their faith. Just as they had done in Newport, they kept their business closed on Saturday and out of respect for their Christian neighbors, on Sunday as well. Although Aaron Lopez traveled extensively in an effort to protect his business interests, he apparently found life in Leicester pleasant. As he wrote to a friend:

> Since we left [Newport], my principal object was to look out for a spot, where I could place my family, secured from sudden allarms and the cruel ravages of an enraged enemy. Such a one I have hitherto found in the small inland township of Leicester in the Massachusetts Bay, where I pitch'd my tent, erecting a proportionable one to the extent of my numerous family on the summit of an high healthy hill, where we have experience'd the civilities and hospitality of a kind neighborhood, and moved in the same sphere of business I have been used to follow, which, although much more contracted, it has fully answer'd my wishes, and you know, my friend, when that is the case, it never fails of constituting real happiness.

But Newport remained on their minds, and to raise the spirits of his ailing father-in-law, as well as the desire of his wife to see old friends, Aaron decided they would take a trip to Providence in the last week of May 1782. A few miles northwest of Providence they stopped to water their horses at Scott's Pond in Smithfield. His wife, father-in-law and some other family members rode in a carriage, while Aaron drove a light, two-wheel sulky. Apparently unaware of the pond's depth, Lopez allowed his horse to enter the water to drink. Suddenly the animal fell into a deep spot, and as the sulky began to sink, Aaron jumped out of it and into the pond, perhaps in an effort to save his horse. Despite a lifetime spent as a shipping owner, he had never learned to swim, and drowned before he could reach the shore. His body was later recovered, and buried in the Jewish cemetery in Newport, a few blocks away from the synagogue he had helped to build.

Aaron Lopez's death proved a severe blow to both the Jewish community and to Newport itself. Still a

relatively young man, his entrepreneurial talents and wide business connections might have provided a catalyst for the town, and his presence would certainly have served as a basis around which the Jewish community and Congregation Yeshuat Israel could have rebuilt. Without him, the Jewish community continued to dwindle, as its younger members left to seek greater opportunity in New York and elsewhere. Jacob Rodriguez Rivera continued to do business in Newport, but the "old gentleman" died in 1789, and the census the following year showed only seven Jewish families remaining in Newport, two of them headed by widows, Abigail Polock and Sarah Lopez.

The damage done to Newport by the British did not generally extend to houses of prayer, although several "meeting houses" had been converted to hospitals during the war. British policy and superstition kept troops from vandalizing places of worship. Neither Trinity Church nor the Friends' Meeting House suffered, and the British also spared the synagogue. Because of the damage done to some of the public buildings, the synagogue after the Revolution served as a temporary meeting place for the general Assembly, some of the courts, and a town meeting.

With its *hazzan* gone and so few Jews remaining, communal worship continued, but on a greatly reduced basis. Uriah Hendricks of New York, on a visit to Newport in 1789 found that the small group of men who gathered in the synagogue read the weekly portion of the Torah not from one of the scrolls but from a printed book. They may have done this because they lacked a *minyan*, or because none of the remaining Jews could read the vowel-less script of the Torah scrolls, an ability their former *hazzan* possessed.

The community had lost not only its *hazzan*, but also its *schochet*, its ritual butcher, and so had to do without kosher meat. After the British left, however, the Jews of Newport experienced a revival. A new *schochet* appeared, a man named Hillel Judah, who seems to have stayed there for most of the 1780s, for in 1787 Newport

Right: George Washington (1732–1799), 1799/1800.

Letter from President George Washington to the Hebrew Congregation in Newport, Rhode Island, in response to the letter from Moses Seixas, August, 1790.

"May the Children of the Stock of Abraham, who dwell in this land, continue to merit and enjoy the good will of the other Inhabitants; while every one shall sit in safety under his own vine and fig tree, and there shall be none to make him afraid."— *George Washington, 1790* merchants shipped kosher beef to Suriname. At some point a Rabbi Calveres arrived in Newport, and for a few years served as *hazzan* of the synagogue. In 1790, the congregational account books kept by Moses Seixas listed 30 different names, including several members of the Lopez family, and the census that year indicated that 20 Jewish families, numbering nearly 100 persons, again lived in Newport.

Yet within a year death and emigration reduced this number to the point that the synagogue was closed except for sporadic events, and all but two of the torah scrolls went to New York for safe-keeping by Shearith Israel. Eventually the other two scrolls, which Moses Seixas later kept for a time in his house, as well as the proprietary rights to the synagogue building and to the cemetery, also passed to the New York congregation, which still owns them today. In his recollections of Newport, George Channing declared that "the building was left to the bats and moles, and to the occasional invasion, through its porches and windows, of boys who took great pleasure in examining the furniture scattered about."

Channing knew the synagogue building well, and apparently had, like Ezra Stiles, occasionally attended services. The British had taken over the building of his Congregationalist Church as a hospital during the occupation, and after the British left it remained in a state of disrepair. Channing asked if his congregation could use the synagogue for its services, and Moses Seixas, now the *parnas* of Yeshuat Israel, initially agreed. But other members of the community, including Jacob Rivera objected, and when Ezra Stiles, now president of Yale, came back to Newport for a visit, Seixas asked him what to do. Stiles was indignant, and said if he had been in Newport, Channing would never have made that request. With Stiles' backing, Seixas withdrew his agreement.

The Jewish presence, however, would continue to be felt in Newport for many years to come. Moses Seixas would serve as the Master of King David's Lodge No. 1 (later St. John's Lodge, No. 1) and was a founder and Grand Master of the Grand Lodge of Freemasons in Rhode Island, and also as cashier of the Bank of Rhode Island branch in Newport. Isaac Elizer, the man who

had sought naturalization along with Aaron Lopez, returned to Newport, and re-opened his business, as did Jacob Rodriguez Rivera. Their influence in the town, though, would be but a pale reflection of what it had been in the years that preceded the Revolution. There was still one scene to be played out, and its legacy informs us to this day.

On June 20, 1790, Isaac Moses and Solomon Simson, on behalf of Congregation Shearith Israel, sent letters to the Jewish congregations of Newport, Philadelphia, Richmond and Charleston, inviting them to join in a general address to President George Washington. One letter from all the congregations, they believed, "will be less irksome to the President than troubling him to reply to every individual address." The two men noted that this letter should have been sent in 1789, when Washington had been elected president, but local circumstances had prevented that happening. (They also resented the fact that the congregation in Savannah had gone ahead in 1789 and presented its own address to Washington). Moses and Simson suggested that the other congregations submit drafts of what they thought should be in the letter, which could then be edited into one single statement.

Moses Seixas presented the request to the remaining members of Yeshuat Israel, and like the independent Rhode Islanders they were, the Jews of Newport were reluctant to join in with the other congregations. Seixas felt it would be unseemly to address the president, since Yeshuat Israel had never sent any such message to the state governor or legislature. Greeting should have been sent upon Washington's inauguration, and while the Newporters criticized the delay they agreed to cooperate, providing they agreed to the wording of the draft, which they left to the New Yorkers. The other congregations also responded, but with one delay after another nothing had been done when circumstances suddenly gave the Newport congregation an unusual opportunity.

Following his election as president under the new Constitution, George Washington had undertaken a tour of New England in the autumn of 1789, but he had pointedly by-passed Rhode Island, which at that time had not yet ratified the Constitution. After Congress adjourned the following year, Washington decided to go to Rhode Island, which had finally joined the Union, to show that he harbored no grudge against the state. He began his journey on August 15th, accompanied by Secretary of State Thomas Jefferson, New York Governor George Clinton, and other notables. He arrived by packet in Newport on the 17th, stayed overnight, and went to Providence the next day. Time had run out on the Shearith Israel proposal, for the president would soon be in Newport. The arrangements for the reception had to be made, and Moses Seixas managed to present not one, but two, letters of welcome to Washington. One message came from Yeshuat Israel and the other from the Masonic Lodge of which he was Master. Seixas presented these messages on the morning of the 18th, when town leaders and the Christian clergy of Newport also presented addresses to the president. Seixas' letter, as well as Washington's response, are worth quoting in full. Seixas wrote:

> To the President of the United States of America
> Sir:
> Permit the children of the Stock of Abraham to approach you with the most cordial affection and esteem for your person and merits—and to join with our fellow citizens in welcoming you to Newport.
> With pleasure we reflect on those days—those days of difficulty, & danger, when the God of Israel, who delivered David from the peril of the sword, shielded your head in the day of battle; and we rejoice to think, that the same Spirit who rested in the Bosom of the greatly beloved Daniel enabling him to preside over the provinces of the Babylonish Empire, rests and ever will rest upon you, enabling you to discharge the arduous duties of Chief Magistrate in these States.
> Deprived as we heretofore have been of the invaluable rights of free Citizens, we now (with a deep sense of gratitude to the Almighty disposer of all events) behold a Government, erected by the Majesty of the People—a Government which to bigotry gives no sanction, to persecution no assistance—but generously affording to All liberty of conscience, and immunities of Citizenship; deeming every one, of whatever Nation, tongue, or language, equal parts of the great Governmental machine. This so ample and extensive Federal Union whose basis is Philanthropy, Mutual Confidence and Publick Virtue, we cannot but

> acknowledge to be the work of the Great God, who ruleth in the Armies Of Heaven and among the Inhabitants of the Earth, doing whatever seemeth him good.
> For all the Blessings of civil and religious liberty which we enjoy under an equal and benign administration, we desire to send up our thanks to the Antient of Days, the great preserver of Men—beseeching him, that the Angel who conducted our forefathers through the wilderness into the promised land, may graciously conduct you through all the difficulties and dangers of this mortal life; and, when like Joshua full of days and full of honour, you are gathered to your Fathers, may you be admitted into the Heavenly Paradise to partake of the water of life, and the tree of immortality.

Although Washington's responses to most of the addresses were little more than perfunctory, this one seems to have touched him. As he had no time to personally draft responses to all of the addresses, he turned to those accompanying him for aid, and some historians have suggested that Thomas Jefferson, the great champion of religious freedom, either offered or was asked by Washington to frame a response. The final draft reflected the similarity between Jefferson's views and Washington's, and by placing his signature on the document, Washington made its sentiments his own for all time.

> To the Hebrew Congregation in Newport, Rhode Island

> Gentlemen.
> While I receive, with much satisfaction, your Address replete with expressions of affection and esteem; I rejoice in the opportunity of assuring you, that I shall always retain a grateful remembrance of the cordial welcome I experienced in my visit to Newport, from all classes of Citizens.
> The reflection on the days of difficulty and danger which are past is rendered the more sweet, from a consciousness that they are succeeded by days of uncommon prosperity and security. If we have wisdom to make the best use of the advantages with which we are now favored, we cannot fail, under the just administration of a good Government, to become a great and happy people.
> The Citizens of the United States of America have a right to applaud themselves for having given to mankind examples of the enlarged and liberal policy: a policy worthy of imitation. All possess alike liberty of conscience

"Deprived as we heretofore have been of the invaluable rights of free Citizens, we now ... behold a Government, erected by the Majesty of the People ... generously affording to All liberty of conscience, and immunities of Citizenship;" — Moses Mendes Seixas, 1790

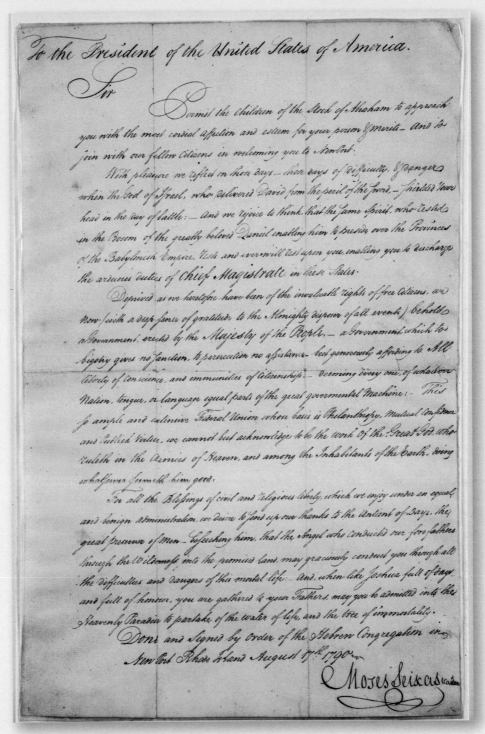

The original letter from Moses Seixas, Warden of the Hebrew Congregation, Newport, Rhode Island to George Washington, August 17, 1790.

and immunities of citizenship. It is now no more that toleration is spoken of, as if it was by the indulgence of one class of people, that another enjoyed the exercise of their inherent natural rights. For happily the Government of the United States, which gives to bigotry no sanction, to persecution no assistance, requires only that they who live under its protection should demean themselves as good citizens, in giving it on all occasions their effectual support.

It would be inconsistent with the frankness of my character not to avow that I am pleased with your favorable opinion of my Administration, and fervent wishes for my felicity. May the Children of the Stock of Abraham, who dwell in this land, continue to merit and enjoy the good will of the other Inhabitants; while every one shall sit in safety under his own vine and fig tree, and there shall be none to make him afraid. May the father of all mercies scatter light and not darkness in our paths, and make us all in our several vocations useful here, and in his own due time and way everlastingly happy.

Although this letter carries with it a unique and cherished significance for American Jewry, in many ways it is a treasure of the entire nation. America, as de Tocqueville famously wrote, had been "born free," unfettered by the religious and social bigotries of medieval Europe. The United States, although initially founded by emigrants from the British Isles, had well before the Revolution become a haven of many peoples from continental Europe seeking political and religious freedom and economic opportunity. The new nation recognized this diversity for what it was, one of the country's greatest assets, and took as its motto *E Pluribus Unum*—Out of Many, One—not just many states, but, implicitly, many peoples as well.

A century and a half before Washington's letter, Roger Williams had first held up the then-radical idea of a full separation of church and state. Although Williams preached the idea of a Christian Commonwealth, he believed that the state should tolerate difference of belief and practice rather than force any person to worship God in a particular, officially authorized manner. Washington now took the next step.

The United States did not espouse mere toleration, but full liberty of conscience. Freedom of religion in the United States had risen to the level of an inherent natural right, protected by the Constitution, and now part of those inalienable rights mentioned in the Declaration of Independence. All the country asked in return was that everyone, of whatever faith—Catholic, Protestant, Jew, or even those with no faith at all—assume the responsibilities of good citizenship. The idea of full religious liberty was as radical in 1790 as it still is in far too many parts of the world, but it has been one of the bases of American life. The separation of church and state, and with it the freedom of religion enshrined in the First Amendment to the Constitution, has made the United States a beacon of hope to oppressed peoples everywhere.

6

CHAPTER | The Caretakers

Judah Touro (1775–1854), about 1850.

Panoramic Map of Newport, Rhode Island, 1878.

"We, the undersigned, Jewish residents of the City of Newport, State of Rhode Island, assembled in conference on the 28th day of May, 1893 to make known that we have formed, and by their presents declare, that we have formed the Jewish congregation, the name and title of which shall be known as the Congregation Jeshuat Israel. … We pledge ourselves to work in harmony to advance the interest of this congregation and the teaching of God's holy law, and to exemplify to our coreligionists the good teachings of those who helped build this ancient home of worship to the glory of God.

— *Preamble to the founding charter of Congregation Jeshuat Israel — May 28, 1893.*

{ CHAPTER 6 }

The Caretakers

THERE IS A CERTAIN IRONY IN THAT WITHIN A FEW YEARS after President Washington's address to Newport Jewry, the community itself died out. The business heart of Rhode Island shifted to Providence, and Newport never again provided the economic opportunity it had in the golden era prior to the Revolution. In 1822, the last member of the Jewish community left Newport.

Yet the story takes a strange twist. The beautiful synagogue designed by Peter Harrison passed into the control of Congregation Shearith Israel in New York, and its trustees had the wisdom not to dispose of the building. Then, thanks to the generosity of the sons of Isaac Touro and the devotion of a Newport Quaker family, the synagogue building remained in satisfactory repair and the cemetery was preserved. The building itself did not sit completely unused; we have stories of people coming back to Newport, or émigrés and their descendants asking to be buried in the cemetery. And so it stood ready to receive the wave of late 19th-century Jews who would come to live in Newport.

Jews returned to Newport only irregularly in the middle years of the 19th century, but since the 1880s there has been a continuous Jewish presence in the city. By the turn of the twentieth century, the synagogue once again contained worshippers, and in 1946 the appreciation of its historical importance as well as architectural beauty led the federal government to designate the building as a national landmark.

Newport recovered slowly from the Revolutionary War. Little or no work existed in the city, and the inflation resulting from paper money made it difficult for anyone to do business in the state. Shipping interests moved to Providence and Boston, while Newport's warehouses

remained empty, wharves rotted, and its once thriving shipyards and rope works stood silent. During the administration of John Adams, an undeclared war with France found some Newporters sending their ships out as privateers and, while a few of them may have found profit in the enterprise, for most ship owners the period from 1790 until after the end of the War of 1812 constituted nothing but one economic downturn after another. Then in September 1815 came the "Great Gale," a hurricane that flooded waterfront property under several feet of salt water, destroyed all the boats in the harbor, and heavily damaged houses several hundred feet inland. The advent of steam railroads connected many towns in Connecticut and Massachusetts to growing markets, but no trains came to Newport, leaving its economy even more isolated.

Best estimates show that the Jewish community at the time that Washington visited in the summer of 1790 counted six or seven families (around 15 households), consisting of perhaps 100 souls. As we noted, it enjoyed the services of a *schochet* as well as a successor *hazzan* to Reverend Touro, and no doubt its members hoped that as the economic fortunes of Newport increased, so would theirs. Alas, this would not happen. Newport's economy remained depressed, and slowly the Jewish merchants, especially the younger generation, left the town to seek their fortunes elsewhere. A majority went to New York; the rest settled in Philadelphia, Charleston and other cities with growing Jewish populations, as well as abroad.

The community evidently lost its new *hazzan* around then, and laymen took over leadership of the services, with apparently disastrous results. The services lost their beauty. Confusion reigned as to how certain rituals should be performed, and attendance dwindled even further. The congregation owned only one old, cracked *shofar*, the ram's horn that is sounded on the High Holidays, but even worse, no one knew how to blow it. When Uriah Hendricks, a member of Shearith Israel in New York, a regular visitor to Newport attended services in 1790, the form and conduct of the ritual so offended him that he left the building and refused to return.

Apparently the congregation did not lack financial resources, for Moses Seixas indicated about this time that Yeshuat Israel faced no monetary problems; services and maintenance of the building could be supported just from the dues paid annually by the members. In fact, he wrote to the president of Congregation Mikveh Israel in Philadelphia asking whether traditional practice of asking offerings at each service might be abolished, since they did not need the money.

By the time of Washington's visit, it appears that services had already become sporadic at best. Apparently some services did take place, because when Moses Levy wrote his will in 1792 he stipulated, "There shall be a Solemn Prayer said for me in said Synagogue yearly and every year on the evening or day of Kippur or Atonement." He would hardly have written that if the synagogue had been closed. Nonetheless regular services ceased around this time, although the exact date is unknown.

A number of sources indicate that title to the synagogue building and the cemetery passed to Shearith Israel in 1790, but whether this took place legally or as a matter of expediency is also unclear. When Moses Levy died in 1792, he left to Moses Seixas, as part of his estate, his personal share of ownership in the synagogue building and the land on which it stood. The deed of that land had been made out to Levy, Isaac Hart and Jacob Rodrigues Rivera. Hart had left his one-third share to Rivera, who had bequeathed what now amounted to two-thirds ownership "to and for the sole use, benefit and behoof [sic] of the Jewish Society of Newport, to be for them reserved as a place of Public Worship forever."

By the end of the 18th century, the "Jewish Society of Newport" consisted of a handful of members of the

Seixas, Rivera, Lopez and Levy families, and their numbers continued to dwindle. [In 1894 the descendants of these last members of the Newport community made the necessary transfer of legal title to Shearith Israel, which for the next several decades oversaw the affairs of the synagogue and cemetery.]

Somehow, throughout the first two decades of the 19th century the Jewish presence in Newport persisted. Abraham Rodriguez Rivera inherited membership in the Redwood Library from his father, and appears to have been an active member, as were Joseph and Samuel Lopez. Benjamin Seixas enlisted in the War of 1812 as the clerk of the Newport Volunteers, and an Abraham Massias also served in the army. Moses Seixas helped organize the Bank of Rhode Island, and served as cashier of the Newport branch from 1795 until his death in 1809. When he died on a visit to his daughter and her family in New York in November of that year, his body was brought back to Newport, the funeral conducted in the synagogue, and his remains interred in the Hebrew cemetery.

Whatever their individual accomplishments, those who remained could not bring the organized Jewish community back to health. On May 5, 1816, Stephen Gould noted in his diary that the "Widow Lopez and family, also Widow Rivera, aged 96, sailed for New York." A few months later he entered the fact that "Moses and Jacob Lopez went to New York— This was probably a prospecting tour for the purpose of consultation as to the probabilities of bettering their condition." They apparently returned, because we learn that on March 18, 1822, Jacob Lopez died in Newport, and on October 5, 1822, Gould wrote the following in his diary: "Moses Lopez, the last Jew, left Newport for New York."

Before the final exodus, Shearith Israel of New York acted to preserve what it could. In 1818 the congregational minutes noted that there had been no services in the Newport synagogue for "a great number of years." Two scrolls of the Torah that Shearith Israel had loaned to the Newport congregation had been for more than 20

Right: Abraham Touro (1774–1822), about 1817.

years in the home of Moses Seixas, and after his death under the charge of his widow and his son, Benjamin Seixas, and Shearith Israel sent word to Seixas asking that the scrolls be returned to New York. However, "if hereafter a *Minyan* shall be in Newport, R.I., and a request be made for a further loan of said Seapharim [scrolls] that the Trustees of the Congregation, will again loan the same for the purpose of being used in the Synagogue." Apparently another 15 years would pass before Benjamin Seixas relinquished the Torah scrolls to Shearith Israel, but the New York congregation kept its word, and a half-century later when Jews again held services in Newport, it restored the Torah scrolls to the sanctuary of Yeshuat Israel.

In December 1833, *Hazzan* I.B. Seixas accompanied the remains of the widow of Joshua Lopez, née Rebecca Touro, by steamship from New York to Newport so that she could be interred in the old cemetery. A contemporary newspaper account of the event noted, "This is the first time for the last 40 years that the ceremony of the Jews has been performed in the Synagogue." By then, however, her brother Abraham had taken an important first step in ensuring the preservation of the Newport synagogue where their father had officiated as *hazzan* before the Revolution.

Following the death of Isaac Touro in Jamaica in 1784, his widow Reyna moved with her three small children—Abraham, Judah and Rebecca—to Boston and to the home of her brother, Moses Michael Hays. Upon her death a few years later, Hays raised the children as his own. Rebecca married a son of Aaron Lopez, while the two brothers became extremely successful merchants. They also became models of philanthropy both for their own times and ever since.

When the first Jews landed in New Amsterdam in 1654, the colony's governor Peter Stuyvesant wanted to expel them at once, but mindful of the Jewish investors in the Dutch West India Company, decided to consult first with the directors. Stuyvesant's letter reached Amsterdam in early 1655, and immediately drew a protest from the city's Jews. On April 26, 1655, the West India Company's directors ordered their governor to allow the Jews to stay, provided, among other conditions, that "the poor among them shall not become a burden to

the company or to the community, but be supported by their own nation." From that time forward, Jews in the New World have made it a point to take care of their own, setting up, over the course of three and a half centuries, a social service system that parallels and in some cases exceeds that of the larger society. Giving charity, however, is not unique just to those who settled in North America, but is one of the central tenets of the Jewish religion.

In the Bible, God tells the Israelites that "If there be among you a needy man, one of your brethren…thou shalt not harden thy heart nor shut thy hand from thy needy brother; but thou shalt surely open thy hand unto him and shall surely lend him sufficient for his need in that which he wanteth." (Deut. 15: 7-8) Both Isaiah and Ezekiel considered charity an essential element of a life of piety, and Proverbs describes the "woman of valor" as one who "stretcheth out her hands to the poor." (Prov. 31:20) The rabbis preached *tzedakah*, which means not only "charity" but "righteousness" or "justice," for in the Jewish religion one of the highest forms of righteous behavior is helping those in need. The Talmud developed an elaborate code of charitable conduct, defining not only who qualifies as a recipient but also how and how much should be given. There was a great emphasis on not embarrassing the recipient, and many rich men took great pains to hide their charitable work; while this could not always be done, it remains the ideal.

Thus both Abraham and Judah Touro would have been raised with the understanding that along with good fortune came the responsibility to use one's wealth for the benefit of the community. Fortunately for Newport, the two brothers, who had been born there during the time of their father's service, had fond memories of the town, and both in their lifetimes and in their wills, gave generously to ensure the preservation of the synagogue and the maintenance of the cemetery.

Abraham stayed in the Boston area, but visited both New York and Newport frequently. Although not a member of Shearith Israel, he turned out to be one of its most generous patrons in the first half of the 19th century. The trustees of the synagogue had a plaque erected "to the Memory of Abraham Touro whose practical efforts to cherish the Religion of his Fathers were only equaled by his munificence which showered its Blessing without sectional distinction."

When Abraham's mother Reyna died at the relatively young age of 44, she had been interred in the Hebrew Cemetery in Newport with a modest marker. In 1814 her son Abraham replaced it with a more elaborate yet still dignified marker, noting not only her passing but also that of her husband and his father, who lay buried in Jamaica.

In 1820 Abraham Touro erected a brick wall built around the old cemetery at a cost of $1,000, to replace the by then dilapidated wooden fence that had been erected in the previous century. The deed required that the cemetery be enclosed, or the land would revert to its original owner. A brick wall would provide greater durability for the enclosure. On June 22, 1822 he wrote to his "esteemed friend" Stephen Gould, the trustee for the "historic relics" of the Jews in Newport:

> *I hope by this time the work is completed, and done to please all, I mean you and Myself. If it should turn out that it is not finished, I wish you would have it done soon, or let me know when it will be…If any friends call on thee for the keys to see the places, you will have the goodness to attend them, or let them have the keys with their promise to close all again and return them to you.*

In fact the work had almost been completed, but Abraham Touro never got to see it. While sitting in his carriage viewing a military parade on October 3, 1822, the fire of the artillery frightened his horses and they bolted. Touro leaped from the carriage, and in doing so broke a leg. The wound became infected, and he died two weeks later. By his request, his body was brought to Newport and interred in the Hebrew cemetery next to his mother.

In his will, Abraham left a sum of $10,000 (the equivalent of over $153,000 in current dollars) to the State of Rhode Island, "for the purpose of supporting the Jewish Synagogue in that State, in Special Trust to be appropriated to that object, in such manner as the said Legislature together with the Municipal Authority of the Town of Newport may from time to time direct

and appoint." He also left $5,000 for the maintenance of the street in front of the synagogue, and from that time the street has been called Touro Street. In the act of the legislature accepting the bequest, for the first time the house of worship of the Hebrew Congregation of Newport is referred to as "Touro's Synagogue." Despite the acceptance of the gift, apparently the assembly did nothing about it immediately, and it required several petitions from a New York committee, as well as from Rebecca, Abraham Touro's sister, before the assembly began paying the caretaker for his work and the costs of repairs. By 1884, despite the absconding by a trustee of more than $4,600, the fund had grown to $23,800, with the income used to keep the synagogue building in good repair. Today the fund has grown to nearly two million dollars, and (despite the doctrine of "separation of church and state") is still controlled and administered by the state of Rhode Island.

As we noted earlier, the fact that the Touro Synagogue survived is due in large measure to the devotion of the Gould family of Newport. James Gould had been a successful merchant in Newport during its golden era, and his Quaker family continued to live there throughout the 19th century. Somehow, his son Stephen became the keeper of the "historic relics of the Jews," and although acting as an agent for the owner, Shearith Israel, appears to have had relatively little oversight from New York. Stephen managed the relatively extensive renovations that took place in 1828, when Benjamin Howland's painting of the Ten Commandments was completed and mounted above the synagogue's Torah ark. Upon his death, his sons David and Nathan assumed the responsibilities, and his grandson, also named Nathan, copied all of the tombstone inscriptions, both in Hebrew and in English, in 1872.

Among the Goulds' responsibilities were opening the synagogue and arranging for the occasional burials that took place, usually of the children of the older Newport Jews. They also opened the building and cemetery for visitors, and in 1852, Nathan Gould opened the gates of the burial ground to one of America's greatest writers, Henry Wadsworth Longfellow, who two years later immortalized it in "The Jewish Cemetery at Newport." In turn, in 1871, Emma Lazarus would write a response to Longfellow's poem, "In the Jewish Synagogue in Newport."

The two poems are very similar in some ways. Both are of old memories in a place now abandoned and silent. But Longfellow was an outsider, and to him Jews were an exotic, a peculiar people, a relic of history, and in his last stanza implies that they are a nation that will be no more. Emma Lazarus is also sad that the synagogue is empty, but this is a place of her people, and the memory of the community is still alive, the synagogue still holy even when empty.

When Longfellow died in March 1882, Lazarus wrote an appreciation that she read at a meeting of Young Men's Hebrew Association in New York. While praising Longfellow's "tender humanity" and the beauty of his verse, she notes that Jewish readers "will not be willing to accept the concluding stanzas." She noted the growing influence of Jews in western Europe, the "frightful wave of persecution" in the east, and the beginnings of a major immigration of Jews to America. "All this proves them to be very warmly and thoroughly alive, and not at all in need of miraculous resuscitation."

Indeed, although the usual story is that no Jews lived in Newport in the six decades following the departure of Moses Lopez, Longfellow's assertion that "gone are the living" seems a bit exaggerated. As Newport gained a reputation for being a summer resort, there appears to have been a colony of summer Jews from New York who lived in the vicinity of Catherine Street. In 1850 enough Jews took up summer residence that Touro Synagogue reopened for services during the season, and we have a record of that event:

This Sacred Edifice was reopened for Divine Services on Sabbath the 25th day of Ab 5610, corresponding with the 2/3 days of August 1850, after a suspension of about Sixty years by a few of the children of Israel temporarily sojourning in this City, and thus continued during the warm season whilst the requisite number remained to form a Congregation.

In the absence of a professional Reader the Hebrew services on this occasion (commencing on Friday evening) were performed by several individuals, (including

descendants of some of the old Congregation of the 2d, 3d, and 4th generations) under the superintendence of the Revd. Morris J. Raphall, (late of Birmingham, England) Lecturer and preacher to the Congregation B'nai Yeshurun, New York, who delivered a Discourse in English, and read the portions of the sacred law of Moses appropriate to the day.

The names of those present on this interesting occasion, and subsequently during the season participating in the holy worship, conducted in accordance with the ritual of the Spanish and Portuguese Jews as had always prevailed in the Synagogue are hereto subjoined—

The services on the first Sabbath were conducted by Revd. M. J. Raphall
Theodore I. Seixas
Samuel Cohen of New York
Asher Kursheedt
Gustavus I. Isaacs
And those of the succeeding Sabbaths by Revd. Eleazar Lyons of Boston, Asher Kursheedt, acting as Parnass (President) and Joshua Isaacs as Secretary.

The appended list of congregants for that season included 23 from New York, three from Charleston, two from Savannah, and one each from Philadelphia, New Orleans, and Germany. Apparently not enough Jews assembled in the subsequent years to form a *minyan*, but vacationers occasionally asked for and received permission to hold private services in the building. Beyond that, some Jews may have become year-round residents, since the records for 1856–1857 list ten Jewish names

Just four years before Longfellow published his poem, American Jewry had mourned the death of Judah Touro in New Orleans. The second son of Isaac and Reyna, Judah used to say that he had been born to the roar of cannon announcing the Declaration of Independence from Great Britain. Brought up along with brother and sister by his uncle, Moses Michael Hays, he also chose a career in business, and like his brother made a great success of it. Unlike Abraham, however, Judah chose to go south, and in early 1802 landed in New Orleans. He opened a small store on St. Louis Street, and before long he became a successful shipper, importer, and dabbler in real estate.

He did not speculate, nor did he ever give up his store, which although not the most profitable of his various ventures nonetheless remained at the core of his empire. From the beginning, he seems to have been a generous man, and as he grew wealthier so did the size of his contributions, although he took as much care as possible to hide that part of his character from the limelight. To give but one example, he read in a newspaper that Amos Lawrence had pledged $10,000 to complete the long-deferred monument to the battle of Bunker Hill, providing someone else would make a like contribution. Touro immediately sent a check for $10,000 to the committee, asking them not to give his donation any publicity. His generosity became known anyway, and at the dedication of the Bunker Hill monument a poem, reputedly by Oliver Wendell Holmes, linked Touro and Lawrence, noting that both Christian and Jew shared in the credit.

In 1815, on the eve of the battle of New Orleans, Touro enlisted as a common soldier, and while carrying shot and shell from the magazine to Humphrey's battery, a cannonball struck him in the leg, leaving him severely wounded and unconscious on the battlefield. Although left for dead, his good friend and fellow merchant, Rezin David Shepherd, found him and brought him to safety and medical care, and after a long convalescence Touro recovered fully.

Like his brother, Judah remained devoted to Newport, even though he had been a lad of five when his father had left the town for New York. He learned that the Redwood Library's portico badly needed repair, and sent a check to cover the costs. When his sister died, he had a beautiful monument erected above her grave in the Touro cemetery, where he himself would eventually lie, along with his mother, brother, and sister. When he learned that the brick wall that his brother had built around the Newport cemetery had begun to decay, he had it replaced with a beautiful granite and wrought iron enclosure designed by the Boston architect Isaiah Rogers, which is still in place. This action led the City Council of Newport in July 1842 to have a similar enclosure built around the synagogue itself, and asked Rogers

to design it so that it corresponded both to the cemetery fence and the portico of the Harrison building.

Touro died on January 18, 1854, and when the terms of his will became known, the publicity he had shunned all his life now came to full focus on him, as newspapers all over the country carried stories on their first pages about the unique bequests he made. The will, drawn up just before his death, had more than 60 separate clauses, in which he left varying sums of money to a host of charitable institutions both Jewish and non-Jewish. Nearly every synagogue and Jewish eleemosynary institution in the country, as well as several in Palestine, received gifts, as did a number of friends and relatives. None of the gifts carried any restrictions, and in terms of the total amount of money given, he actually left more to Christian groups than to Jewish ones.

As the Rev. Theodore Clapp noted, "I have never heard of but one coreligionist in the United States, who can be compared with Mr. Touro, as regards the liberality of his benefactions to his own church; and he bestowed nothing on other denominations. But Mr. Touro gave more to strangers than to his brethren. With a generous profusion, he scattered his favors broadcast over the wide field of humanity. He knew well that many of the recipients of his bounty hated the Hebrews, and would, if possible, sweep them into annihilation."

Early on in the will he made clear his intention to be buried in Newport. He left $3,000 to the Redwood Library for building repairs and the purchase of books, and he gave $10,000 to the City of Newport for the purchase and improvement of another of Newport's famous buildings, the Old Stone Mill, with the property to be kept as a public park. Article 55 read as follows:

I give and bequeath ten thousand dollars for the purpose of paying the salary of a Reader or Minister to officiate in the Jewish Synagogue of Newport, Rhode Island, and to endow the Ministry of the same, as well as to keep in repair and embellish the Jewish Cemetery in Newport aforesaid; the said amount to be appropriated and paid, or invested for that purpose in such manner as my executors may determine concurrently with the corporation of Newport aforesaid, if necessary. And it is my wish and desire, that David Gould and Nathan H. Gould, Esq., of Newport

Henry Wadsworth Longfellow

"The Jewish Cemetery at Newport."

How strange it seems! These Hebrews in their graves.
Close by the street of this fair sea-port town;
Silent beside the never-silent waves,
At rest in all this moving up and down!

The trees are white with dust, that o'er their sleep
Wave their broad curtains in the south-wind's breath,
While underneath such leafy tents they keep
The long, mysterious Exodus of Death.

And these sepulchral stones, so old and brown,
That pave with level flags their burial-place,
And like the tablets of the Law, thrown down
And broken by Moses at the mountain's base.

The very names recorded here are strange,
Of foreign accent, and of different climes;
Alvares and Rivera interchange
With Abraham and Jacob of old times.

"Blessed be God! for he created Death!"
The mourners said: "and Death is rest and peace."
Then added, in the certainty of faith:
"And giveth Life, that never more shall cease."

Closed are the portals of their Synagogue,
No Psalms of David now the silence break,
No Rabbi reads the ancient Decalogue
In the grand dialect the Prophets spake.

Gone are the living, but the dead remain,
And not neglected, for a hand unseen,
Scattering its bounty, like a summer rain,
Still keeps their graves and their remembrance green.

How came they here? What burst of Christian hate;
What persecution, merciless, and blind,
Drove o'er the sea,—that desert, desolate—
These Ishmaels and Hagars of mankind?

They lived in narrow streets and lanes obscure,
Ghetto or Judenstrass, in mirk and mire;
Taught in the school of patience to endure
The life of anguish and the death of fire.

All their lives long, with the unleavened bread
And bitter herbs of exile and its fears,
The wasting famine of the heart they fed
And slaked its thirst with marah of their tears.

Anathema maranatha! Was the cry
That rang from town to town, from street to street;
At every gate the accursed Mordecai
Was mocked, and jeered, and spurned by Christian feet.

Pride and humiliation hand in hand
Walked with them through the world, where'er they
went;
Trampled and beaten were they as the sand,
And yet unshaken as the continent.

For in the back-ground, figures vague and vast
Of patriarchs and of prophets rose sublime,
And all the great traditions of the Past
They saw reflected in the coming time.

And thus forever with reverted look,
The mystic volume of the world they read,
Spelling it backward like a Hebrew book,
Till Life became a Legend of the Dead.

But ah! what once has been shall be no more!
The groaning earth in travail and in pain
Brings forth its races, but does not restore,
And the dead nations never rise again.

"In the Jewish Synagogue at Newport."

Here, where the noises of the busy town,
The ocean's plunge and roar can enter not,
We stand and gaze around with fearful awe,
And muse upon the consecrated spot.

No signs of life are here: the very prayers,
Inscribed around are in a language dead,
The light of the "perpetual lamp" is spent
That an undying radiance was to shed.

What prayers were in this temple offered up,
Wrung from sad hearts that knew no joy on earth,
By these lone exiles of a thousand years,
From the fair sunrise land that gave them birth!

Now as we gaze, in this new world of light,
Upon this relic of the days of old,
The present vanishes, and tropic bloom
And Eastern towns and temples we behold.

Again we see the patriarch with his flocks,
The purple seas, the hot sky o'erhead,
The slaves of Egypt—omens, mysteries—
Dark fleeing hosts by flaming angels led.

A wondrous light upon a sky-kissed mount,
A man who reads Jehovah's written law,
'Midst blinding glory and effulgence rare,
Unto a people prone with reverent awe.

The pride of luxury's barbaric pomp,
In the rich court of royal Solomon—
Alas! We wake: one scene alone remains
The exiles by the streams of Bablyon.

Our softened voices send us back again
But mournful echoes through the empty hall;
Our footsteps have a strange, unnatural sound,
And with unwonted gentleness they fall.

The weary ones, the sad, the suffering,
All found their comfort in the holy place,
And children's gladness, and men's gratitude
Took voice and mingled in the chant of praise.

The funeral and the marriage, now, alas!
We know not which is sadder to recall;
For youth and happiness have followed age,
And green grass lieth gently over all.

And still the shrine is holy yet,
With its lone floors where reverend feet once trod.
Take off your shoes as by the burning bush,
Before the mystery of death and God.

Emma Lazarus

aforesaid, should continue to oversee the improvements in said Cemetery and direct the same; and as a testimony of my regard and in consideration of services rendered by their said father, I give and bequeath the sum of two thousand dollars to be equally divided between them, the said David and Nathan H. Gould.

All told, Touro's estate amounted to some $433,000 in cash bequests as well as non-cash bequests, such as land, that amounted to another $70,000, a total of over $500,000, the equivalent of over $10,630,000 in our day. While there have been richer men who have left greater sums of money, it is fair to say that no one has touched so many different groups, Jew or Christian, institution or individual, as Judah Touro did. His funeral on June 6, 1854, at the same synagogue over which his father had presided for many years, drew an immense crowd, with over 150 Jews from all over the country, many of them representing the congregations and other agencies to which he had been so generous. The coffin was carried in a long procession through the town, and thousands of people lined the route. The Rev. J. K. Gutheim of New Orleans conducted the ceremony in Hebrew and English, and in the audience were not only fellow rabbis from the leading synagogues, but also a large number of Christian clergymen.

The City Council accepted the provision of his bequest, and with the exception of $200 paid annually to the Goulds in their role as caretakers, invested the money, so that when the time came for a new migration of Jews to establish a new congregation in Newport, the Touro Fund provided the money necessary to hire a rabbi. Unfortunately, the city managed the fund poorly, and for many years invested it in short-term, low interest bonds. Not until 2000 did the city finally adopt a different policy, and pooled the Touro fund with other trust funds. There is currently between $175,000 and $200,000 in the fund.

Judah Touro's continuing and wide-spread influence is still with us. In 2001 a new bridge from Boston to Charlestown was named the Leonard P. Zakim bridge, to memorialize a Jewish Bostonian who worked for the Anti-Defamation League. There were protests that it should be called the Bunker Hill Bridge because Jews had nothing to do with Bunker Hill. News that Judah

Touro had paid a large sum toward the completion of the Bunker Hill monument in Boston helped silence the critics.

The revival of a Jewish community in Newport began around 1870, when a number of mainly immigrant Jews from eastern Europe arrived. For the most part they lived within walking distance of the synagogue, and a number of them opened businesses on and around Thames Street. While a few took up itinerant peddling, most opened small shops and sold clothing or dry goods. During the summer season a number of Jewish tailors opened up temporary shops in Newport, catering to the growing influx of summer visitors, and after 1883 to the officers at the newly established Newport Naval Station.

By 1881 a sufficient number of permanent residents wanted to reopen the synagogue and make it once again a living house of God. The building itself was in satisfactory condition, thanks to the bequest of Abraham Touro and the loving oversight of the Gould family. In 1858, $4,455.46 had been paid out of the Touro Fund, most of it for repair and maintenance of the building. In 1866 the Fund paid for the repainting of the synagogue, and in 1872 the Goulds arranged for gas lighting to be installed. Apparently enough visitors wanted to enter the building that the City Council employed a permanent custodian, at the rather meager salary of $50 a year. With a building awaiting their use, the members of a would-be congregation petitioned the Newport City Council in 1882 for permission to become the regular users of the synagogue, and to bury their dead in the cemetery. The trustees of Shearith Israel, the legal owners of the facilities, now had to decide what steps to take.

In August of that year, the trustees of Shearith Israel dispatched one of its members, the prominent attorney Gratz Nathan, as well as the religious leader of the congregation, Dr. H. Pereira Mendes, to investigate. They appeared before the City Council, which, recognizing Shearith Israel's legal status regarding the synagogue, turned over the petition to the two men for further action. The Jews of Newport then asked Shearith Israel not only for the use of the building, but also for a permanent rabbi, to be paid out of the fund established by Judah Touro.

The trustees met on September 18, 1881, and replied that they would be willing to make the synagogue available and would arrange for a *hazzan* to conduct Sephardic services on the high holidays of that and ensuing years. Since the synagogue had none of the ritual objects needed for the services, Shearith Israel would provide the scrolls of the law that they had held in safe-keeping for Yeshuat Israel for more than six decades, as well as a *shofar* (ram's horn), and candlesticks. The trustees demurred, however, about utilizing the Touro Fund to hire a rabbi, and put off that decision until "there shall be a sufficient number of permanent residents to maintain the Services throughout the year in accordance with the principles, and form of Orthodox Judaism as contemplated by the term of the will of the late Judah Touro." The decision of Shearith Israel appears wise, since not enough Jews lived in the city at the time to form a self-supporting congregation, and after the 1881 High Holiday services—the first since the end of the 18th century—the torah scrolls and other objects went back to New York.

The arrival of more Jews in Newport during the next several months led to a renewed interest in forming a congregation, as well as a religious school in which the community's children could be taught. In December 1882, the leaders of the group addressed a petition to Shearith Israel, and also to the Newport City Council. The latter group acted first, passing a resolution authorizing the permanent reopening of the synagogue and the employment of a minister to conduct services and supervise religious education who would be paid out of the Touro Fund. In addition, the Council identified the person that the local Jewish community wanted to call to Newport to become their spiritual leader: the Reverend Abraham Pereira Mendes of London, the father of the rabbi of New York's Shearith Israel.

The record is silent about whether the London Mendes had been approached by the Newport Jews, or if they thought that by using his name it would make Shearith Israel more favorable to their cause. In any event, it turned out that Mendes, born in Jamaica in 1825, was willing to move to Newport. The trustees of Shearith

Israel approved the new request, with the proviso that the services there must always follow the Sephardic ritual. They also restated their legal rights to the building and cemetery. Mendes duly arrived in the country, took up residence in Newport, and on May 25, 1883, presided over the reconsecration of the Touro Synagogue. Apparently the congregation's demand for a minister's services outweighed its actual need, since Mendes, a few months after his arrival, petitioned the City Council for permission to be absent from the city from November to April because of the lack of a *minyan*.

Although the congregation under Rabbi Mendes had been using the Touro Synagogue building since 1883, its occupancy of the building was at times problematic. The Jews of Newport found themselves in a rather unique situation: they had requested and acquired the use of the building and the burial ground through a lease with the legal owners—the trustees of New York's Shearith Israel. The Newporters, nearly all of whom were Ashkenazim from central and eastern Europe, clearly chafed under some of the conditions of the agreement. The Newport congregation, founded on 28 May 1893 as Congregation Jeshuat Israel and incorporated one year later, repeatedly petitioned both the Newport City Council and Rhode Island legislature to gain more control over its own affairs. In turn, for the next decade, Shearith Israel on several occasions sent representatives to Rhode Island to reassert its legal rights. In addition, although Shearith Israel did not have direct control over the funds established by Abraham and Judah Touro, it kept an eye on the expenditures and insisted that the monies be used only for the purposes designated by the donors—maintenance and repair of the synagogue from the bequest from Abraham, and the salary of the rabbi from Judah—and not for the general needs of the congregation.

Rabbi Mendes died in 1893, after serving in Newport for ten years. By then a split had occurred in the congregation that erupted openly after his death. Some congregants remained willing to follow the restriction placed on them by Shearith Israel, while others wanted to act more independently. The issue of following Orthodox or Reform Judaism's practices—a question that divided many other congregations in the United States at this time—did not play any role here; both sides were committed to traditional Judaism but differed on its practice. The main difference seems to have been friction between Jews from Germany and those from eastern Europe, Poland and Russia. As in so many other American Jewish communities at this time, the German Jews considered themselves better educated and more cultured than the recent immigrants who looked less assimilated and spoke Yiddish. Finally in 1894 the Rhode Island legislature granted a charter incorporating the congregation in Newport known as Jeshuat Israel (the name meant the same as Yeshuat Israel although the spelling differed). To safeguard the interests of Shearith Israel, it made a permanent allotment of four seats on the synagogue's board of trustees to the New York congregation.

Despite efforts by the new rabbi, Dr. David Baruch, to mend the split, the antagonisms continued, and broke out again after Baruch's death in 1899. The rebellious faction, composed primarily of eastern European Jews and calling itself the "Touro Congregation," held its services at 11 Coddington Street, and for the high holy days used some rooms at the old City Hall. It hired the Rev. E. M. Meyer to be its religious leader, while Jeshuat Israel, dominated by the Germans, elected the Rev. Moses Guedelia to be theirs. Since the Touro congregation had far more members than Jeshuat Israel, the Newport Town Council voted to pay the salary of its leader out of the Touro Fund. With this action a war broke out involving three parties—the Touro Synagogue Congregation, Congregation Jeshuat Israel, and Congregation Shearith Israel—that lasted more than three years.

Having secured recognition from the city as the rightful beneficiaries of the Touro Fund, the Touro Congregation group also wanted possession of the synagogue itself, which remained under the control of Congregation Jeshuat Israel and its sponsor, Shearith Israel. The eastern European Jews claimed that the building was, for all intents and purposes, empty and abandoned. Fischel David, one of the leaders of the Touro Congregation bloc, approached John C. Burke, a prominent Newport attorney and later a state judge. Burke checked the laws, and finally concluded that there was no legal way to gain possession of the building. "I determined that there was no method by which they could go to court and get any relief," Burke later recalled, "and

the only way to handle the matter would be just forcibly to enter the Synagogue, have a religious gathering and a Rabbi on the altar, and carry on their religious rites."

Burke's theory rested on the notion that "the Jewish society" to whom Jacob Rodriguez Rivera had willed his two-thirds ownership in the building "as a place of public worship forever" meant the Jewish community of Newport, and that the deed of trust in which the building and burial grounds had been given to Shearith Israel had no force whatsoever. By taking physical possession of the building, the matter could then be tried in a court of equity in which Shearith Israel would have to defend its claim. He would be able to put forward his theory that the Touro group, constituting the majority of the Jewish population in Newport, rightfully owned the building in its capacity as the current "Jewish society."

On the evening of the first day of Passover, Fischel David, Burke, and others went to the synagogue, broke the locks, entered, lit some candles, and began services. Burke had earlier spoken with Chief of Police Benjamin Richards and the assistant attorney general, Charles H. Stearns (later chief justice of the Rhode Island Supreme Court), informing them of the plan, to which they gave their assent. After he watched David enter the building, Burke went home to have his dinner, and while there heard all the alarm bells and church bells ring. His wife, a native Newporter, said she had heard something like that when she was a girl. It was a riot call.

Apparently the custodian of the synagogue, Eugene Schreier, had seen the break-in and called the police. He asked them to remove the men from the building because they had no right to be there. When police officers tried to do this (apparently they did not know Chief Stearns had approved the break-in), a riot ensued. Fischel David, acting under Burke's direction to resist any efforts at eviction, had been grabbed by a police officer and had promptly bit the officer's thumb. Burke, invoking Stearns' name, managed to have the police depart and all of the men who had been detained released. The invaders, as per Burke's plan, kept services going day and night so as not to vacate the premises and allow the members of Jeshuat Israel to regain control.

Ocean House, Newport, Rhode Island. J. G. Weaver, Proprietor, about 1857.

The anger and disdain of the German Jews to their co-religionists can be seen in a letter written by Sarah Schreier to a local newspaper two days after the break-in. She condemned what she called the "Russian-Polish element" in town. "Into this holy place" she wrote, "this place so dear to me, broke a lawless band masking in the cloak of religious feeling like wolves in sheep skins. They blasphemed the name of the Almighty by breaking into His Holy Temple: a deed no good Jew or Christian would stoop to. No words can express how low was the act; an act punishable in olden times by stoning the offenders at the door of the Temple." But Sara Schreier also went on to note that after the death of the Rev. Mendes, attendance had dropped considerably, until the congregation consisted of only a few families like her own.

Burke's strategy seemed to be working, and Fischel David went into court in an effort to force Shearith Israel to turn over title of the synagogue and cemetery to the Touro Congregation faction. Shearith Israel promptly sent one of its trustees, Louis Napoleon Levy (the brother of Jefferson Levy, the man who had saved Jefferson's home, Monticello, after the Civil War) to defend Shearith Israel's rights and confirm them in law once and for all. The two sides argued the case before the Federal Circuit Court of Rhode Island in late 1902. The court handed down its decision on January 10, 1903, completely vindicating the rights of Shearith Israel in the Newport synagogue.

Despite victory in the courts, Shearith Israel's trustees recognized that circumstances had changed drastically in Newport, and some solution had to be found to the problem. Moreover, the invaders had held continuous possession of the synagogue since the previous April, and even Shearith Israel had to recognize that if there was a "Jewish assembly" in Newport, these were its members.

The New Yorkers approached Burke and indicated that although the court decision confirmed their rights, they sought reconciliation. So did the Newporters, and as a first step the two factions agreed to phase out the Touro Congregation, and that all Jews would be part of Jeshuat Israel, housed in the Touro Synagogue. After a series of conferences, the trustees of the two congregations—Shearith Israel in New York and Jeshuat Israel in Newport—signed an agreement, calling for the Newporters to lease the building at an annual rental of one dollar a year. Once again the key part of the agreement centered on the mode of ritual. Jeshuat Israel would use and maintain the Touro Synagogue to conduct "religious services according to the ritual, rites, and customs of the Orthodox, Spanish, and Portuguese Jews at this time [1903] practiced in the Synagogue of the Congregation Shearith Israel in the city of New York." Shearith Israel also retained a veto over the appointment of a minister by Jeshuat Israel.

The reconciliation among the parties had actually begun shortly before, when Jacob M. Seidel agreed to become minister of the congregation, the first Ashkenaz rabbi in Newport. Since then Jeshuat Israel has continued to pray in the Sephardic mode, although its rabbis and nearly all of its members are of Ashkenazic lineage. The contract between Shearith Israel and Jeshuat Israel has held for more than a century.

CHAPTER **7** Preserving the Traditions

Touro Synagogue after the latest renovations, 2008.

Touro Synagogue National Historic Site Campus (2012). Right to left: Touro Synagogue (1763), Patriots Park, Loeb Visitors Center (2009) and Visitors Center Annex (Barney House, 1704).

{ CHAPTER 7 }

Preserving the Traditions

IN THE 20TH AND 21ST CENTURIES, NEWPORT'S JEWISH community increased, diminished, evolved and reinvented itself, reflecting changes through all of American social, economic, and political life. When the synagogue was reopened in 1883, there were fewer than 100 Jewish families in Newport. That was soon to change when Newport, like every other American Jewish community, felt the influence of the "Great Migration." In the next 40 years, by 1924, over two million Jews emigrated to the United States. Most of the new immigrants, coming from northern and eastern Europe, generally followed Ashkenazi cultural and religious practices. Although the majority stayed in the New York area, over the following decades, individuals, families, and larger groups dispersed all over North America. As elsewhere, Newport's Jewish population increased both in numbers and in participation in community life.

Congregation Jeshuat Israel remained the central focus but, between 1880 and 1920, Newport could boast of at least 20 Jewish organizations. Some were chapters of national organizations and others were formed locally for social and philanthropic reasons. The increase in Jewish population in and around town led to the founding of a second Orthodox congregation in 1915, Temple Ahavis Achim, also known as "The Bull Street Shul". Shortly after, the two congregation jointly opened a United Hebrew School; a YMHA [Young Men's Hebrew Association] was founded in 1919. As immigration quotas came into effect and the waves of new arrivals slowed, many of the less vibrant organizations dropped away. By 1924, there were only eight identifiably Jewish institutions, including the two congregations, the YMHA, the Council of Jewish Women, and the Judah Touro Lodge No. 998 of B'nai Brith.

During this period of growth and after World War I, the maintenance and repair of the synagogue building remained an important focus for the Jewish community. One of the provisions of the 1903 agreement between Shearith Israel and Jeshuat Israel involved maintaining the historical integrity of the synagogue building. In 1905 Jeshuat Israel wanted to make some alterations and expand the side building that housed the religious school. Congregation Shearith Israel immediately responded from New York: "This Board would not consent to any alteration of any description in that historic edifice." The Jeshuat Israel Congregation in Newport had to be content with minor repairs but did manage in 1909 to re-outfit the furniture in the sanctuary, installing "158 chairs, cushions for settees, carpets [and cuspidors]" in the sanctuary.

The community was not isolated. As news came from "the old country" of pogroms and other violent anti-Semitic activities in Europe the local focus often shifted to international concerns. Congregation Jeshuat Israel created relationships with the Anti-Defamation League, Hillel (the Jewish college student organization), and Zionist organizations in support of victims and the affected overseas communities. Newport's Jewish organizations joined with the rest of the town during the First World War by sponsoring blood drives for the war effort, creating social and religious outlets for sailors at Naval Station Newport, and offering general support for members of the military from within the congregation.

After the war, Jewish congregations all over America saw membership and activity start to decline. Newport's congregations were fortunate to have a fairly stable membership (many of whom were related to other members and many had ancestors who had been members of the founders of the new congregation in 1883). All were tied by their commitment to Touro Synagogue as an historic building worthy of great care and protection.

So in 1925, at a time when other small-town Jewish communities were struggling, the congregation at Touro Synagogue began fundraising for a Jewish community center to be located on Touro Street directly across from the synagogue's main entrance. Serendipitously, the city announced plans to demolish the old Levi-Gale Mansion (built at the East end of Washington Square in 1833/34]) to make way for a new Newport County Courthouse. The local congregation raised the $25,000 needed to acquire the building, including a contribution of $5,000 from Shearith Israel in New York. Immediately, the board of Jeshuat Israel purchased the Levi-Gale house and arranged to move it to the new location three blocks away. Movers cut the structure in two and, using oxen and sleds, transported each half up Touro Street to the corner of Division Street. The Levi-Gale house was seated on a new foundation, reassembled, and was dedicated in 1926. Known as the "Jewish Community Center," the building is still used as the offices, educational and social activity annex for the Jeshuat Israel congregation.

By the 1930s Irving Warshawsky had been hired as the director of the Jewish Community Center, and with the guidance of Dr. Morris Gutstein (rabbi of Congregation Jeshuat Israel from 1932 to 1943), the new JCC teemed with active groups serving all sectors of Jewish Newport. Rabbi Gutstein was also the first of the congregation's rabbis to do extensive historical research on the colonial Jewish community and their congregation, Yeshuat Israel. He was author of *The Story of the Jews of Newport* (New York: Jewish Publication Society, 1936) and two other books: *The Touro Family of Newport* and *Aaron Lopez and Judah Touro*. His was the vision to start a formal process to have Touro Synagogue and its history recognized at the national level for both the historic events and symbolism it embodied. Rabbi Gutstein was eager to communicate the history, architecture, and meaning of the oldest extant synagogue in the United States to the widest possible public.

World War II brought a burst of activity to all of Newport. Rabbi Jules Lipschutz stepped into the spiritual leadership role in 1943 and served through the war until

1949. Jeshuat Israel volunteers established programs for Jewish men and women serving at Newport's naval base, began regular visits to the Naval Hospital, and started a USO in the Community House, open to all servicemen, regardless of religious affiliation—the hostesses (and dance partners) were the young women of the Jewish community.

Lipschutz picked up Gutstein's mission to have the Synagogue recognized, seeking new resources for synagogue preservation. The legacies left by Abraham and Judah Touro (among the first for "historic preservation" purposes) were sufficient for minor repairs and for a minimal salary for a rabbi and custodian, but no more. To keep up with the maintenance requirements of an 18th-century building, other sources of funding needed to be found.

So, when Congress passed the Historic Sites Act of 1935, which allowed nationally significant venues to be designated as a "National Historic Site," the Congregation and its supporters saw the potential for long-term benefits. If designated as such as site, the Secretary of the Interior and the owners of Touro Synagogue could sign a cooperative agreement that focused on resource stewardship. At the prompting of congregational board members, Arthur Hays Sulzberger, publisher of the *New York Times* and a descendant of Benjamin Mendes Seixas (buried in the Colonial Cemetery at Newport), wrote in February 1944 to Harold Ickes, Secretary of the Interior, suggesting that the National Park Service identify an appropriate Jewish property for recognition as part of an overall effort to mark important historic churches throughout the original thirteen colonies. Touro Synagogue would be an obvious choice, combining superb architecture with significant historical value.

The Park Service moved rapidly and by the end of the month had completed its field inspection of the site. In the spring of 1945, it recommended that President

Right: Levi-Gale Mansion being moved, 1925. The building was cut in two. Then teams of oxen were used to pull each half of the building from Washington Square up the three blocks to the corner of Division and Touro Streets.

National USO award given to the Ladies Auxiliary of Congregation Jeshuat Israel. *This honors their hospitality to US military service personnel during World War II. The Touro Lodge of B'nai Brith received a similar award.*

Harry S. Truman approve the designation of Touro as a National Historic Shrine (later changed to National Historic Site). Truman approved the designation on April 19, 1945. On March 5, 1946, an impressive number of federal, state and local officials and representatives of the nation's Jewish communities gathered to mark the event. There they received a message from President Truman that states, "The setting apart of this historic shrine as a national monument is symbolic of our tradition of freedom, which has inspired men and women of every creed, race and ancestry to contribute their highest gifts to the development of our national culture."

Identification with the federal government and the National Park Service certainly helped the synagogue's preservation, but more was needed. Members of the congregation and supporters of the Synagogue from New York and elsewhere banded together in 1948 to form the Society of Friends of Touro Synagogue (now the Touro Synagogue Foundation) to aid in the maintenance and upkeep of the buildings and grounds, and to publicize the history of the Touro Synagogue. The Foundation began holding its annual "George Washington Letter Reading" to mark the anniversary of George Washington's historic pronouncement on religious freedom. This event, held annually in August, has a long tradition of distinguished speakers reading the

Washington letter, such as Supreme Court Justice Ruth Bader Ginsberg, actor Charlton Heston, and Senator Claiborne Pell.

After the war, congregational life settled into a quieter mode. In 1949, Rabbi Theodore Lewis left his home congregation in Dublin, Ireland and became the rabbi for Touro Synagogue. He remained in Newport for 36 years. Lewis brought Touro Synagogue to national attention, even appearing on the television show "To Tell the Truth" as "the only Irish-born rabbi serving in the United States." He revitalized the congregation and the Hebrew School, the Men's and Women's Clubs, B'nai Brith, youth groups and sports teams, all contributing to the continued health of the congregation. Rabbi Lewis also took up the banner of promoting Newport's Jewish history. His personal *cause célèbre* was to have the U. S. Post Office issue a stamp honoring Touro Synagogue. His dream came true when the Postmaster General unveiled the design for a 20-cent, first class stamp in 1980. Commemorating Touro as both a national historic building and a symbol of religious freedom, the stamp was released to the public on August 22, 1982 during the annual George Washington Letter Reading weekend.

In addition to promoting Touro's role in American history, the congregation and later the Friends of Touro Synagogue have been acutely aware of the preservation and conservation efforts required to maintain an 18th-century structure as both a viable house of worship

Supreme Court Justice Ruth Bader Ginsburg receives the Judge Alexander Teitz Award on George Washington Letter Reading Day, 2004.

for an active congregation and as a tourist attraction. Throughout the 1900s, there were many renovations and restorations to the historic structure. However, in the 1950s a forward-looking party of interested individuals gathered in an effort to expand and to truly bring the site into the modern age.

By 1955, the condition of the synagogue had deteriorated to the point that the Friends of Touro Synagogue needed to solicit additional private funds to renovate and repair the foundation, interior and exterior of the building. William Zeckendorf was appointed as chair of the Touro Restoration Committee. Zeckendorf's participation attracted many notables to the

Rabbi Theodore Lewis discussing the history of Touro Synagogue with a visiting group of Catholic nuns, about 1960.

Board of Directors of The Society of Friends of Touro Synagogue, including financiers and politicians like Carl M. Loeb, Senator Herbert H. Lehman, Morris Morgenstern, Henry Alexander of Atlanta, Judge Edgar J. Nathan Jr., Dr. David de Sola Pool (rabbi of Congregation Shearith Israel in New York), and Arthur Hays Sulzberger. Loeb, Lehman, Alexander, Nathan, and Sulzberger are all relations by blood or marriage to

the original community of Yeshuat Israel who built the Newport synagogue in 1763.

Their initial fundraising goal was fairly modest, but when land adjacent to the synagogue came on the market, the restoration plan was expanded to include a new "Patriots Park" honoring Jewish patriots from the colonial era. The budget was increased to $300,000 to enable the purchase of the additional land and the creation of a park that would allow an unobstructed view of and approach to the building. Target date for the completion of the restoration was 1958, but it wasn't until December 1960 that the renovated synagogue was dedicated and the park followed in 1965.

By 1961, it appeared that both the congregation and the synagogue were on relatively firm ground, but changes in the nature of Newport's Jewish community brought yet another period of evolution.

Since its 1903 agreement with Shearith Israel, Touro's congregation was required to use and maintain the synagogue to conduct "religious services according to the ritual, rites, and customs of the Orthodox, Spanish, and Portuguese Jews at this time practiced in the Synagogue of the Congregation Shearith Israel in the city of New York." Shearith Israel also retained a veto over the appointment of the Newport rabbi. In 1961, these requirements as well as a general trend in American Jewish life towards more liberal forms of worship prompted 35 Newport families from both Jeshuat Israel and Ahavis Achim to form Temple Shalom, the Conservative Congregation of Newport County. The new and growing congregation originally met in a synagogue in Newport itself. However, in October 1974 their downtown facilities located on Thames Street were destroyed by arson. Through the strong efforts of their membership and with the support of the local community, the congregation kept on and soon relocated, building a new house of worship in Middletown, just north of Newport. The new building was dedicated in 1978 and a new Hebrew school building was opened in 1988.

Congregation Jeshuat Israel took this moment to re-dedicate itself to its commitment to the vibrancy of the religious community associated with Touro Synagogue. The congregation remains Orthodox, worshiping according to the Sephardic ritual, yet they have managed to be quite progressive in their structure and operations. It is true that men and women are separated during services—yet in 1999, Rita Slom was among the first women in the United States to be elected as president of an Orthodox congregation's board of directors. She has been followed by several other women in that role.

Congregation Jeshuat Israel now has approximately 140 member families and sponsors various religious, educational, social, and cultural programs and activities. Lifecycle events including Bar/Bat Mitzvot and weddings are frequently held at the historic Synagogue. All services and religious activities are now under the direction of Rabbi Dr. Marc Mandel, the spiritual leader of Touro Synagogue. Mandel succeeded Rabbi Mordecai Eskowitz, who served from 1999 to 2012, a period of significant renovation and expansion of the Touro Synagogue National historic site campus.

The commitment of the members of Touro Synagogue's spiritual community will see it into the future. But the preservation requirements of a 250-year-old building continue to increase. In the 1990s, the congregation realized that it was time to do a more substantial renovation than was done in 1956-60. With the help of grants from the National Park Service, the National Trust for Historic Preservation, and other public and private funding sources, they began on a top-to-bottom $3.5 million restoration project.

Special care had to be taken not to alter the internal or external appearance of the Peter Harrison building. Existing windows were removed to an off-site workshop and restored, thousands of bricks had to be repaired by hand, and a modern rain gutter and fire safety system—now required by the city's building code—had to be installed, the gutter hidden beneath the fragile slate roof, and the fire system tucked away in the ceiling.

As difficult as the restoration of the old building may have been, the work on the artifacts inside proved an equally challenging task. Howard and Mary Newman, the owners of Newmans Ltd. of Newport, and their staff took apart the chandeliers and other metal fixtures, which had tarnished over the years and parts of

which had been bent or broken. The chandeliers are not matched sets, so each one had its own challenges. The *ner tamid*, the Eternal Light that burns in every synagogue in the world, had at some point been electrified, but in 2006 its red glass chimney was cracked and years of polishing had left layers of dried and cracked cream that hid the natural beauty of the fixture. Moreover, because it is an electric appliance, the fire code required a grounding screw, which the restorers concealed in a support chain. The *chanukkiah* (the nine-candle *menorah* lit on Chanukah), candlesticks, the old mahogany wall clock gifted in 1769, and the *rimonim* (the silver Torah finials), some of which dated to the original construction in the 18th century, all had to be carefully disassembled, cleaned, repaired, reassembled and polished. The results are breathtaking. For this work, the Rhode Island Historical Preservation and Heritage Commission, at its annual meeting in 2007, recognized the Touro Synagogue and the construction contractor "for their painstaking restoration of the oldest synagogue in America" and gave them one of its annual Project Awards.

In the 1990s the Friends of the Touro Synagogue also began exploring the possibility of constructing a welcome center for visitors to gather before entering the synagogue. Here, before taking a tour of the historic synagogue, visitors could get information about colonial Newport in general, its Jewish community in particular, and specifically explore the full history of the Synagogue. The congregation approached Ambassador John L. Loeb Jr. with a proposal for such a center and he was intrigued. Loeb was well-known in Jewish philanthropic circles, and he had personally underwritten a number of historical publishing projects and museum exhibits, including a history of the Levy family and its stewardship of Jefferson's Monticello, as well as an exhibition and catalogue of paintings of American Jews in the colonial and early national periods. During the Zeckendorf fundraising drive, the Ambassador's father, John Loeb Sr., and uncle, New York governor Herbert Lehman, had made him aware of the synagogue and its importance and introduced him to his ancestral connection to Newport's Jewish community.

Loeb and the Friends of Touro Synagogue and the Board of Congregation Jeshuat Israel began exploring

Touro Synagogue and Patriots Park before the 2009 renovation. The center pedestal by the wall supports a bronze plaque of President George Washington's 1790 Letter to the Hebrew Congregation in Newport. This photograph, taken around 1980, shows the synagogue as seen from the north-west. Until the opening of Patriots Park (1965), this view had not been seen since colonial times.

the possibility of a full Visitors Center to be built as the gateway to the synagogue historic site. On behalf of the congregation, Loeb purchased the land and two buildings (Gray Typewriter Company, circa 1950 and the historic Barney House, circa 1704) at the bottom of the hill just west of the synagogue and adjacent to Patriots Park. After the Gray Typewriter building was razed, there would be just enough space for a new visitor's center. The building could not be too large, lest it overwhelm Peter Harrison's jewel box of a synagogue or the historic Barney house next door.

Ground was broken for the Visitors Center in 2007, right after the synagogue was rededicated. Ambassador Loeb assembled a team of architects, historians,

curators and builders to take on the tasks involved. Loeb personally oversaw the selection of the architects and plans, went through the zoning process, and worked with the historical exhibits team to determine what issues should be covered in the display. He helped to design the landscaping for the newly restored Patriots Park that sits between the Visitors Center and the synagogue. He also built a gate through Judah Touro's wall, thereby connecting the synagogue with the park and the Visitors Center.

While tours of the synagogue have been given since the synagogue became a National Historic Site in 1946, the interactive exhibits in the new Ambassador John L. Loeb Jr. Visitors Center, enhance and enlarge the scope of the visitor experience at Touro Synagogue by further explaining how Newport and the Rhode Island colony became the focal points for the concepts of religious liberty, tolerance, and the separation of church and state in colonial America. Visitors are introduced to the roles of the Founding Fathers (Roger Williams, Washington, and Jefferson) as key figures in the dissemination of these concepts through the story of Washington's Letter to the Hebrew Congregation of Newport. Other displays examine the history of Jews in Colonial and Revolutionary War America; and present the history of Touro Synagogue to the present.

Since, the Loeb Visitors Center opened in 2009, it has won several awards for architecture and landscaping. Each year, thousands of visitors explore the Center's exhibits as part of the overall experience of visiting the synagogue national historic site. The renovation of the synagogue, the restoration of Patriots Park, and the construction of the Visitors Center have all contributed to revitalization of the neighborhood around the Touro campus.

Congregation Jeshuat Israel and the Touro Synagogue Foundation should be recognized for their foresight and commitment to the preservation of Peter Harrison's architectural gem and their dedication to keeping the message of American religious freedom alive and in the public mind. Throughout the year, the congregants of Jeshuat Israel are joined in worship at Touro Synagogue by Jews from around the nation and the world, and tourists have made Newport their vacation destination specifically to visit Touro. The Newport Jewish community is preserving and maintaining the historic building for use by others even as it continues to serve as the home for their own personal worship. With the help of supporters from around the United States, these caretakers maintain a legacy that belongs to the nation and the world.

The synagogue stands as a monument to the tenacity of a small number of Sephardic and Ashkenazic Jews fleeing persecution to make a new home for themselves in the 17th and 18th centuries. It is also a monument to an idea. When Roger Williams founded Rhode Island, he envisioned a "Christian commonwealth," but one that would be hospitable to the members of other faiths.

What started as mere tolerance eventually developed into the philosophy embedded in the First Amendment of the Constitution, that government shall do nothing to interfere with an individual's free exercise of religion, nor establish an official religion. To accomplish this goal, Williams also put forward that other foundation of religious liberty, the separation of church and state.

All Americans have been the beneficiaries of these ideals, but perhaps none so much as those professing their faith as Jews. After nearly two millennia of persecution, the Jews who came to Newport did not find an earthly

The Ner Tamid (1765), or Eternal Light, in Touro Synagogue.

paradise. They still faced discrimination, but on a scale so remote from what they had suffered in Europe as to make it virtually inconsequential. Moreover, no laws prohibited them either from practicing their religion or becoming economically successful. Their exchange of letters with the nation's first president produced one of the most important documents in the history of American religious liberty: George Washington's pledge that there would be "to bigotry no sanction." While

this promise resonates with Americans of all faiths and creeds, it has a special significance for the Jewish community which has lived here in freedom for more than three and a half centuries. Never a large community at any time, the Jews of Newport have left to other Jews and to other Americans a living embodiment of what religious liberty means. Touro Synagogue is a physical manifestation of their dreams, their hopes, and their legacy.

HONORED IN PATRIOTS PARK (FOR EACH OF THE ORIGINAL 13 COLONIES)

Connecticut ....Myer Myers *(1723–1795)*
Delaware ....Solomon Bush *(1753–1795)*
Georgia ....Mordecai Sheftall *(1735–1797)*
Maryland ....Jacob Hart *(1746–1822)*
Massachusetts..Moses Michael Hays *(1739–1805)*
New Hampshire ....Abraham Cohn *(1832–1897)*
New Jersey..Aaron Louzada *(1693/5–1764)*
New York..Gershom Mendes Seixas *(1746–1816)*
North Carolina ....Jacob Mordecai *(1762–1838)*
Pennsylvania..Haym Salomon *(1740–1785)*
Rhode Island ....Aaron Lopez *(1731–1782)*
South Carolina ....Francis Salvador *(1747–1776)*
Virginia ....Moses Myers *(1752–1835)*

Loeb Visitors Center, East Porch seen from Patriots Park, 2012.

John Loeb's 330 Year Journey to Newport and Touro Synagogue

by Eli N. Evans

Eli N. Evans

Eli N. Evans is a noted American Jewish historian and president emeritus of the Charles H. Revson Foundation in New York City. He graduated from the University of North Carolina (B.A.) and Yale Law School (J.D.) and served as a speech writer on the White House staff of President Lyndon B. Johnson. A native of Durham, North Carolina, Evans is the author of The Provincials: A Personal History of Jews in the South; Judah P. Benjamin: The Jewish Confederate; *and* The Lonely Days Were Sundays: Reflections of a Jewish Southerner, *all of which have received exceptional acclaim and remain classics in the field.*

Of Evans' literary career, Abba Eban, the renowned Israeli statesman and historian stated: "the Jews of the South have found their poet Laureate." When inducted into the American Academy of Arts and Sciences in 2001, he was honored "for his dual contribution to American letters and as a philanthropist of uncommon originality and leadership."

A RECENT PROFILE OF JOHN LOEB JR. IN THE WALL STREET Journal described him as a "scion of a storied family in American finance, tireless philanthropist and patron of culture, Ambassador to Denmark in the Reagan administration, advisor and trustee and board member of a host of institutions, honored recipient of countless service awards and recognitions."

But unstated was John Loeb Jr., the dreamer and time traveler, the ardent partisan of religious freedom, whose journey and imagination begin in 1697, the year his forbearers arrived in America.

I first met John over 30 years ago, when I searched him out when I had been writing about southern Jewish history and came across the fact that this legendary New York City Jewish family had roots in Montgomery, Alabama. John's great grandfather, Alfred Huger Moses, was a leading citizen in that city, having served as a Captain in the Confederate army and, along with his brother Mordecai Moses, been successful in banking and real estate. Mordecai Moses, John's great uncle, also took an active interest in civic affairs and, in 1871, was the first Democrat elected after Reconstruction as mayor of the city, serving honorably for six years. The two brothers were the most respected citizens in the city, where Alfred's daughter – John's revered grandmother, Adeline Moses Loeb – spent her girlhood.

John's grandmother retained a deep Southern accent, even years later as a *Grande dame* in New York City, and was a gifted storyteller who told John and his siblings riveting stories of the accomplishments and struggles of the family before and after the economy in the south collapsed after the Civil War, struggles that continued afterwards through the vagaries of widespread devastation

Adeline Moses Loeb

and a world depression. By the end of the nineteenth century, the Moses family left the south and settled in St. Louis, Missouri.

Now 17 years old and living as part of a family without money, Adeline learned to sew to make her own clothes; use the dexterity of her piano lessons to learn typing and stenography; and helped to run a boarding house with her maiden aunts. One day, she met Carl Loeb, a boarder who was an 18 year old German immigrant, sent by the German parent company of the American Metal Company to work in the American Midwest. He became her destiny, married her, and took her back to New York City to begin a new life that would shape the lives and the fortune of generations of the Loeb family.

These tales touched John deeply, and he wanted to know more. In 1976, he hired a young genealogist named Judith Endelman to trace the story of his family from its beginnings in 1697. He did not know then what an enormous task it would be, lasting off and on for more than eight years.

Endelman wrote of the rarity of the Moses/Loeb story:

In a country as young as the United States, it is unusual to find a family whose ancestors have been in America for over 300 years. When the family is a Jewish family, it is even more unusual. There cannot be more than a handful of families who can make such a claim… Of this handful of families, many died out, migrated, intermarried, and otherwise were lost to history. The family of Adeline Moses Loeb has not been lost to history, even though they were probably in America for a century before the first census was taken.

John discovered many other links from this effort to document his family that would stir his life work and imagination. The family was very daring; each generation moved to a new place, many having large families with as many as 15 children. These stories were collected into a book in 2009, *An American Experience: Adeline Moses Loeb and Her Early American Jewish Ancestors.* Published by The Sons of the Revolution in the State of New York, it brings together a dazzling display of many beautiful portraits, letters, and stories. Among the families was one of John's distant relatives, the famed Judah Touro of New Orleans and Newport, Rhode Island, where some of John's other early family members had moved. John was deeply stirred by the legend of Judah Touro as America's first great philanthropist, a man whose last will and testament was so unusual and far reaching that it made the front page of the New York Times when he died in 1854.

Among those benefiting were Jewish congregations, religious schools, benevolent societies, and hospitals in nineteen American cities; Catholic, Protestant, and other charities in New England; and in New Orleans, numerous churches, hospitals, an orphan home, and an alms house. He even left "$60,000 for various causes in Palestine and $15,000 to help the Jews of China." The will not only broke new ground in its size and global vision but in crucial other ways as well. In 1854, the laws of the time made it difficult to leave money to any recipients other than family members, and there were no tax advantages for charitable giving. Although Judah Touro was America's first great philanthropist, his modest tombstone in Newport is inscribed simply:

The Last of His Name
He inscribed in the Book of
PHILANTHROPY
To Be Remembered For Ever

Among his gifts was substantial support to the oldest synagogue in America, which his father, Isaac Touro, had served as religious leader. It was from the beginning a gem of architectural elegance. It later became known as the Touro Synagogue, named for both Judah and his older brother Abraham Touro, in which a congregation still worships. And John discovered the power of "The Letter": George Washington's letter to Newport's Hebrew Congregation, which was written when Washington and Thomas Jefferson returned from campaigning in Rhode Island for the Bill of Rights and contained the phrase, "To bigotry no sanction, to persecution no assistance."

American Jewish historians knew of the letter, but it was little appreciated by the vast populace in the United States. John believed its ringing message should be enshrined in the pantheon of other documents that serve as building blocks of the American revolution—ranking with the "All men are created equal" clause of the Declaration of Independence; or the opening words of the U.S. Constitution, "We the People of the United States, in order to form a more perfect Union, establish Justice…secure the Blessings of Liberty to ourselves and our posterity." No person in America has done more than John to make the pledge of religious freedom by our first president known across the nation.

It is clear that the stories John heard from his grandmother Adeline were absorbed as part of his life narrative and gave him the inspiration and love that anchors his search for the past. "Grandma Moses" also gave him his Jewish identity and his pride in his Jewish roots. Flowing from these gifts has emerged a plan for a great personal and family legacy. First, John created a teaching and learning center that bears his name on the campus of Touro Synagogue, today the oldest active Jewish house of worship in America, itself named for his Touro relations. The Ambassador John L. Loeb Jr. Visitors Center dramatizes not only the journey of his family over seven generations, but John's personal journey as well. With this Newport project, John has

returned home. In so doing, he completes the circle of his life and of the three centuries of the Moses family.

Religious freedom is America's gift to the world, an example to inspire all humankind with a universal vision of freedom of religion and respect for other faiths that is the basis of the struggle against fanaticism that is casting a dark cloud over the future of human history.

The Founding Fathers broke with history in becoming the first Western nation to turn aside the idea of a state religion, and instead created a nation in which religious belief would be a matter of individual choice and each individual's religious practice would be protected. They put their faith in a religious future for the nation, anchored in the strength of freedom, and they welcomed the resulting diversity of religious practice. The Newport Jewish community and the Touro Synagogue were one of the first beneficiaries of this profound experiment.

Rarely do history, architecture, and the ideals of religious freedom and tolerance converge in a place of such exquisite beauty and design as Touro Synagogue. It is both an active house of Jewish worship and a symbol of the American core values of religious tolerance, civil liberties and the separation of church and state engraved in the American Constitution and the Bill of Rights. This site also honors the Touro family's legacy and, by so doing, the long line of the Moses/Loeb family history as well. They belong together because both the Moses/Loeb family and the Touro Synagogue have experienced almost all of American Jewish history.

The Center is anchored in a singular mission: to deepen every visitor's understanding and commitment to history and the vitality of the idea of religious liberty and the separation of church and state. That is the Center's central purpose and the cornerstone of its design as well.

The mission, as John envisioned it, is to integrate history into the visitor's experience with "a world class center that innovates, attracts, and teaches… to educate future generations and preserve our history." For the approximately 13,000 visitors a year, and the many more who will be attracted to learning about religious liberty and the history of the separation of church and state in

America, John hopes to make the synagogue and the visitor's center "a model and a living landmark to religious freedom."

While Adeline Moses Loeb, the family storyteller, inspired young John with a legacy of tales about his family that made them come alive so vividly, her voice and the stories stayed in his heart all his life and stimulated his interest in American Jewish history. How better to honor her and the long Moses/Loeb line that began in the seventeenth century, at about the same time as the Jewish community in Newport, than by blending the two stories together on the sanctified ground of the Touro campus. They were, after all, Jews cast by history into a search for a haven from religious persecution who found a home in a future nation based on the freedom they yearned for. What they could not foresee was that they had come to a young country for whose destiny they would have to fight. Members of the Moses family fought in every American war for an idea that would be known a century later, as John often emphasizes it, as "*These* United States of America."

In that spirit, John had previously brought his sensibilities and love of history to places and causes that would eventually lead him to Newport. Each time a pathway opened, he ventured down it without turning back. One pathway led him to Montgomery, Alabama, where Adeline was born and her father and uncle helped build the city that was the capital of the state. The family restored the "Mayor's House," which had fallen into disrepair, to its early glory and invited other civic groups to use it. Another pathway led him back to the American Revolution to the Fraunces Tavern in Lower Manhattan in New York City, where General George Washington bade an emotional farewell to his officers of the Continental Army. A portrait of Adeline hangs there. A broader collection of pre-Civil War portraits of American Jews has found a home on a website John has created. It can be found at www.loebjewishportraits.com. For visitors to the Loeb Visitors Center, the portraits are organized on a series of screens—the interactive "Portrait Tree"—along with biographies of the individuals in each portrait. A third pathway led to Newport, Rhode Island, where John became intrigued with the deeper meaning and possibilities of the Touro Synagogue, not only as a house of worship, but also as

a symbol of the roots of freedom of religion and the origins of the separation of church and state that enabled his family and millions more Americans of all faiths to flourish in their new homeland.

John had found his destiny: the place where his dreams would settle, and the vision of a mission that his philanthropy could create and sustain by dramatizing the story of the Bill of Rights—teaching of its history, so that the story of the Washington letter and the First Amendment's unique freedom of religion clause come alive for future generations. He becomes, by the act of his own philanthropy to build the Visitors Center, a visionary who opened more widely the doors of the Touro story to our nation.

John faced the challenge of the architecture of the Loeb Visitors Center with great sensitivity, knowing that all of Newport was watching. He had heard the whispers: will it overpower the synagogue; be very modern in glass and steel and therefore too tall or wide and out of place; or too showy, even garish and with haughty disrespect for its neighbor in such an historic setting; or that it would be too spectacular and possibly even embarrassing in its neglect of its entire neighborhood?

John supervised every decision, called for advice on the best architectural minds and historians and curatorial talent he could find. The result was a spectacular success, lauded by the community and by the architectural world for its modesty and classicism as well as its beauty. It actually makes the old synagogue seem more majestic on the hill, as if the Center is a bride standing at the gateway of the restored "green and grassy Patriots Park" that leads up to her synagogue groom. The park (dedicated to the roles played by Jews in the early development of the U.S.) is graced by the colors of flowers beckoning visitors to walk via a public pathway to learn of the history and the wisdom uttered through the centuries still resonating within the old brick walls of the synagogue. The scene is a reminder of the Biblical reference in Washington's letter that in America, the right to practice religion is not an act of "indulgence of one class of people" for another, but an "inherent natural right." The Constitution promised that "under its protection…Everyone shall sit in safety under his own vine and fig tree, and there shall be none to make him afraid."

David Brussat, the architectural critic of the Providence Journal, noted that the Visitors Center "is obviously a classical building, yet, it is unlike any other. No work of classicism could possibly depart from canon with greater dignity, hence no building could possibly fit into a historic street with greater distinction."

Even before building the Center, John had the vision of taking Washington's message of religious freedom beyond its walls. In 2009, he established the George Washington Institute for Religious Freedom, which today partners with the nation's leading civic education organizations to sponsor national essay contests, train classroom teachers and create a curriculum to use Washington's Letter to teach about religious freedom and the intent of the founding fathers to break with centuries of Western tradition of religion-by-law, putting their trust instead in the common morality of the people to embrace the guarantee of freedom of worship to every citizen.

In a gala parade marking the ratification of the Constitution in Philadelphia on July 4, 1788, President Washington created a symbolic and unexpected moment. The press reported that the crowd of onlookers that lined the streets "saw the clergy of the different Christian denominations with the rabbi of the Jews walking arm in arm." Think of the visual power of that moment: a Protestant minister, a Catholic priest, and a Jewish rabbi linked in unity to celebrate the adoption of the American Constitution.

In approving the Bill of Rights of the U.S. Constitution in 1791, the American people voted for a set of principles that began a fundamental shift in human history and a revolution in human governance still resonating around the world. With freedom of religion, speech, assembly, the press, and petition, the new nation created what scholars have called the "freedom of personal conscience." To underscore the hierarchy of the values at the core of the new nation, the very first sentence in the First Amendment was this simple but dramatic assertion: "Congress shall make no law respecting an establishment of religion, or prohibiting the free exercise thereof."

John has committed the last ten years and much of his philanthropy to that cause. Thus, if family is determined not only by birth but by actions, John will be remembered in Newport and beyond as the third brother to Abraham Judah Touro. They helped sustain the synagogue and gave it a new life. John L. Loeb Jr. has launched the Touro idea into a twenty-first century destiny.

We are grateful to Melvin I. Urofsky, a fine historian who John asked to research and write this book. He brought his customary care, intelligence, and eye for nuance to the task and has written an honest book with a readable prose that will serve Newport and its visitors to the Touro Synagogue National Historic Site for generations to come.

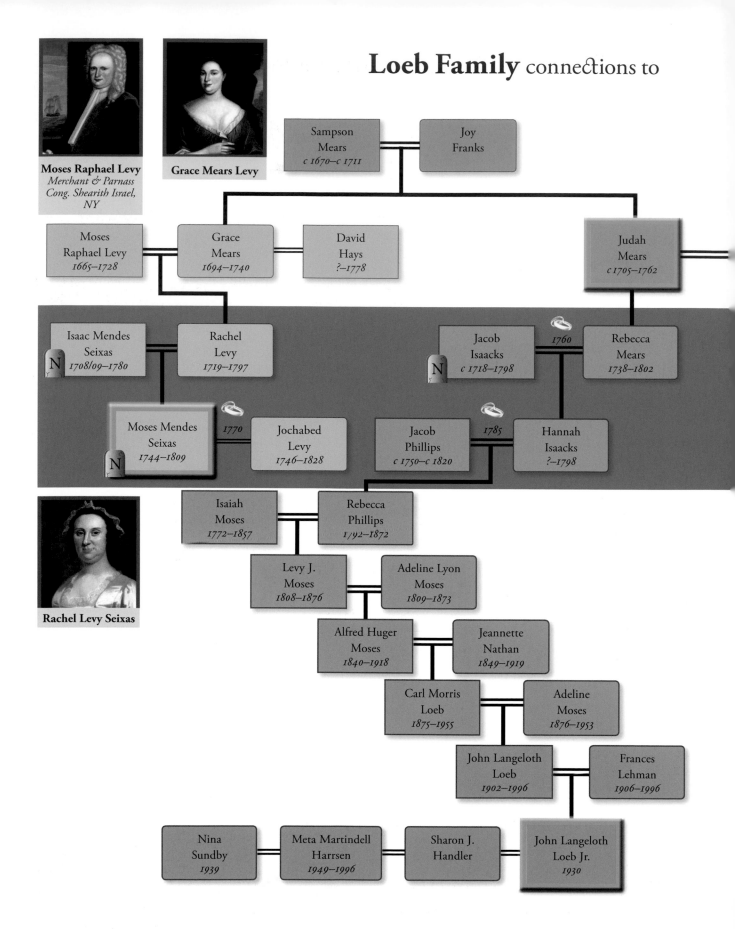

Loeb Family connections to

Moses Raphael Levy
Merchant & Parnass Cong. Shearith Israel, NY

Grace Mears Levy

Rachel Levy Seixas

Sampson Mears
c 1670–c 1711

Joy Franks

Moses Raphael Levy
1665–1728

Grace Mears
1694–1740

David Hays
?–1778

Judah Mears
c 1705–1762

Isaac Mendes Seixas
1708/09–1780

Rachel Levy
1719–1797

Jacob Isaacks
c 1718–1798

1760

Rebecca Mears
1738–1802

Moses Mendes Seixas
1744–1809

1770

Jochabed Levy
1746–1828

Jacob Phillips
c 1750–c 1820

1785

Hannah Isaacks
?–1798

Isaiah Moses
1772–1857

Rebecca Phillips
1792–1872

Levy J. Moses
1808–1876

Adeline Lyon Moses
1809–1873

Alfred Huger Moses
1840–1918

Jeannette Nathan
1849–1919

Carl Morris Loeb
1875–1955

Adeline Moses
1876–1953

John Langeloth Loeb
1902–1996

Frances Lehman
1906–1996

Nina Sundby
1939

Meta Martindell Harrsen
1949–1996

Sharon J. Handler

John Langeloth Loeb Jr.
1930

{ 118 }

Moses Seixas and the Touros of Newport, RI

Judah Mears

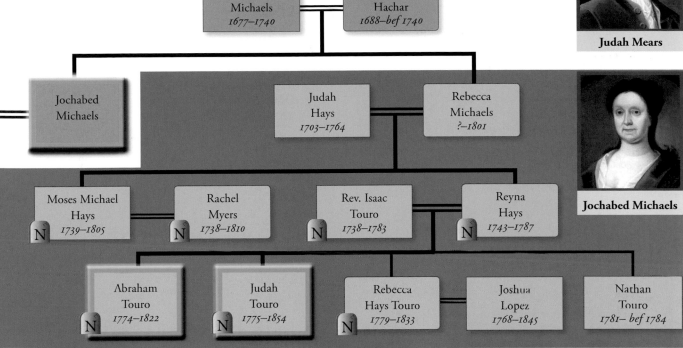

Jochabed Michaels

Moses Michaels
1677–1740

Catherine Hachar
1688–bef 1740

Jochabed Michaels

Judah Hays
1703–1764

Rebecca Michaels
?–1801

Moses Michael Hays
1739–1805

Rachel Myers
1738–1810

Rev. Isaac Touro
1738–1783

Reyna Hays
1743–1787

Abraham Touro
1774–1822

Judah Touro
1775–1854

Rebecca Hays Touro
1779–1833

Joshua Lopez
1768–1845

Nathan Touro
1781– bef 1784

Moses M. Hays
Grand Master Freemason

Isaac Touro
Hazan of Congregation Yeshuat Israel

Abraham Touro
Philanthropist

Judah Touro
Philanthropist

Joshua Lopez
Son of Aaron Lopez

Family who lived in Newport, RI

 year Married in Newport, RI

N Grave or marker in the historic Colonial Jewish Burial Ground, Newport, RI

Direct Line Ancestors & Current Generations

Other Collateral Relations
(aunts, uncles, cousins & their spouses)

For in the back ground figures vague and vast
Of patriarchs and of prophets rose sublime,
And all the great traditions of the Past
They saw reflected in the coming time.

— *Henry Wadsworth Longfellow, 1858*

List of Illustrations and Credits

Suggested Additional Readings

American Judaism: A History.
   Jonathan D. Sarna. New Haven: Yale University Press, 2004.

Ezra Stiles and the Jews, selected passages from his Literary Diary concerning Jews and Judaism
   with critical and explanatory notes.
   George Alexander Kohut. (New York: Philip Cowen, 1902.) [Reprinted from *The American Hebrew*, November,
   1901 to June, 1902. New York: Cameron Press, 1901-1902]

George Washington and the Jews.
   Fritz Hirschfeld. (Newark: University of Delaware Press, 2005.)

The Jews of Rhode Island.
   George M. Goodwin and Ellen Smith (editors). (Waltham, MA: Brandeis University Press, 2004.)

Lopez of Newport: Colonial American Merchant Prince.
   Stanley F. Chyet. (Detroit: Wayne State University Press, 1970.)

The Lustre of Our Country: The American Experience of Religious Freedom.
   John Thomas Noonan Jr. (Berkeley: University of California Press, 1998.)

The Papers of George Washington Digital Edition.
   Theodore Crackel, ed. (Charlottesville: University Press of Virginia, Rotunda.2007.)

The story of the Jews of Newport, two and a half centuries of Judaism, 1658-1908.
   Morris A. Gutstein. Introduction by David De Sola Pool. (New York: Bloch Publishing Company, 1936.)

A Time for Planting: The First Migration, 1654-1820. (The Jewish People in America, Volume 1)
   Eli Faber. (New York: New York University Press, 1998.)

Author Biography

MELVIN I. UROFSKY is Professor of Law & Public Policy and Professor Emeritus of History at Virginia Commonwealth University. He received his B.A. and Ph.D. from Columbia University, and his J.D. from the University of Virginia. Over the years he has held fellowships and grants from the National Endowment for the Humanities, the American Council of Learned Societies, the Virginia Foundation for the Humanities, the American Historical Association and others. He was a Rich Fellow at Oxford University's Center for Jewish Studies, a Fulbright Lecturer at the University of New South Wales Law School in Sydney, Australia, a Rockefeller Foundation Fellow at the Bellagio Center in Italy, and a visiting scholar at Ben-Gurion University in Israel. Under the auspices of the State Department, Urofsky has lectured in Europe, Asia and Australia, and has spoken at many colleges and law schools in the United States. This is the fifty-fourth book Urofsky has either written or edited, several of which have won prestigious awards. He has been the editor for the past nineteen years of the *Journal of Supreme Court History*.

Index

Bold page number indicates an illustration